500

soups

500

soups

Susannah Blake

APPLE

A Quintet Book

First published in the UK in 2007 by Apple Press
74-77 White Lion Street
London N1 9PF

www.apple-press.com

ISBN: 978-1-84543-538-7
QTT.FSO

This book was designed and produced by
Quintet Publishing Limited
6 Blundell Street
London N7 9BH

Senior Editor: Ruth Patrick
Editor: Bridget Jones
Art Editor: Dean Martin
Photography: Ian Garlick
Home Economist: Wendy Sweetser
Creative Director: Richard Dewing
Publisher: Gaynor Sermon

20 19 18 17 16 15 14 13 12 11

Printed in China 1010 Printing International Ltd.

contents

introduction

For as long as humans have been cooking food over a fire, soup has been eaten in one form or another – from the earliest, most basic broths left over from simmering ingredients in a pot of water to sophisticated concoctions, specially created to be served and eaten on their own. Soup is made and eaten all over the world, from Italian *zuppa*, German *suppe* and Balkan *ciorba* to Vietnamese *sup*, Persian *shorba* and Central Asian *sorpa* or *shorpo*. They all share a common texture characteristic, which is that they are all liquid dishes, usually served in bowls.

The bulk of soups are cooked – usually meat, poultry, fish or vegetables simmered in stock – but you will also find uncooked soups, such as Spanish gazpacho and Middle Eastern-style yoghurt soups, for which uncooked ingredients are blended together to make a smooth soup. Soups may be light and clear, such as broth or consommé, rich and creamy, thick and substantial, or chunky and stew-like. Although they are usually savoury, there are also a few sweet soups, including those made with melon, cherry or pear. Sweet soups are generally served in small quantities.

There are many types of soup and an almost infinite number of combinations of ingredients. The flavourings give each soup its own distinctive character. In their wonderful variety, soups can be eaten at almost any time of day, at any time of year. In Asia, they are often served for breakfast. Lighter soups made from vegetables can make a healthy snack between meals, while a more substantial soup can make a sustaining meal in a bowl. Soup is one of the classic first courses on Western menus, served before the main course. It is also perfect for a light lunch or even as a late-night snack before bed. In winter, soups can be fabulous warmers – warding off the seasonal chills – while in summer, chilled soups can be gloriously refreshing.

Wholesome and comforting, plain or complex, sophisticated or simple, whatever kind of soup you're looking for, you're sure to find it here. Packed with delicious recipes and inspiring serving suggestions, this compendium proves that there really is a soup for every occasion.

equipment

Making soups is very easy, and requires very little specialist equipment.

measuring equipment: scales, jugs & spoons
Although most soup recipes are very easy and can be adapted according to the ingredients you have to hand, accurate measuring equipment will prove to be invaluable.

chopping board & knives
Good knives and a board are essential for cutting vegetables, meat, poultry, fish and shellfish. A serrated knife is useful for cutting bread to serve with soup.

vegetable peeler
A vegetable peeler is more practical and efficient than a knife for peeling firm vegetables and fruit such as apples and pears. A vegetable peeler is also a useful tool for paring or shaving fine slivers or slices of Parmesan cheese.

grater
Choose a grater with several different sizes of hole for coarse and fine grating.

garlic press
Although you can crush garlic using the flat blade of a knife, a garlic press is useful and easy to use, particularly if you need to crush several cloves.

cooking saucepan
Choose a large, heavy saucepan with a lid that fits well. This is useful for all stages of cooking soups and for long-simmering stock.

wooden spoons

Useful for stirring ingredients when frying them in the first stages of a recipe, and stirring soup during cooking, or stirring in ingredients at a later stage.

food processor or blender

To make smooth soups, you will usually need a food processor or a blender. There are several different types of blenders, including free-standing and hand-held types. Hand-held blenders are particularly useful for soup-making because they can be used directly in the saucepan, rather than pouring the soup into a food processor or blender, then returning it to the saucepan. Experiment with the settings on a food processor to achieve the best consistency – some processors do not reduce liquids to as smooth a texture as a blender. A traditional *mouli-légumes*, a mechanical sieve, is useful for crushing and puréeing the cooked soup.

strainers

A strainer or sieve is useful for straining soup. There are several types, including a large fine-mesh wire strainer (for sieving food to a purée), a nylon mesh strainer for foods that discolour and a colander for draining large ingredients.

potato masher

A masher can be used for crushing tender cooked vegetables to make a rough textured soup. This technique can also be used if you do not have a food processor or blender.

skimmer

A flat, round perforated utensil – or skimmer – is used to lift scum or froth from stock and soup. A slotted spoon will also do the job, or a large flat-bowled metal spoon can be used.

stocks

A good stock is the essential base for almost every soup. Good-quality stock is now available in supermarkets, delicatessens and food stores, as cubes, bouillon powder, in long-life cartons or fresh from the chiller cabinet. It is worth using a quality stock, bought or home-made, as it will make all the difference to the flavour of soup. Home-made stock can be frozen, so it is worth making a large batch and freezing it in smaller quantities, ready for thawing and using in recipes. Rigid cartons with good lids are practical for storing stock in the freezer.

vegetable stock

2 onions, roughly chopped
2 carrots, sliced
2 celery sticks, roughly chopped
1 bay leaf
2 sprigs fresh thyme
4 fresh parsley stalks
1 tsp black peppercorns
½ tsp salt
1.7 l (3 pts) water
Makes about 1.2 l (2 pts)

Put all the ingredients in a saucepan, add the water and bring to the boil. Reduce the heat and simmer for about 1 hour, skimming off any scum that rises to the surface. Strain the stock through a strainer and leave to cool, then chill or freeze until ready to use.

chicken stock

1 chicken carcass
2 onions, roughly chopped
2 carrots, sliced
2 celery stalks, roughly chopped
2 bay leaves
1 tsp black peppercorns
½ tsp salt
1.7 l (3 pts) water
Makes about 1.2 l (2 pts)

Put all the ingredients in a saucepan, add the water and bring to the boil. Reduce the heat and simmer gently, skimming off the scum occasionally, for about 1½ hours. Strain the stock through a strainer and leave to cool, then chill or freeze until ready to use.

beef stock

900 g (2 lb) beef bones
1 onion, roughly chopped
1 leek, roughly chopped
2 carrots, sliced
1 celery stick, roughly chopped
1 bay leaf

2 sprigs fresh thyme
4 sprigs fresh parsley
1 tsp black peppercorns
$\frac{1}{2}$ tsp salt
1.7 l (3 pints) water

Makes about 1.2 l (2 pts)

Preheat the oven to 220°C (425°F / Gas Mark 7). Put the bones in a roasting tin and roast for about 40 minutes.

Transfer the bones to a large saucepan and add all the remaining ingredients. Bring to the boil, then reduce the heat and simmer, skimming off any scum occasionally, for about 3 hours. Strain the stock through a strainer and leave to cool, then chill or freeze.

fish stock

900 g (1 lb) fish bones (without gills,
  as they are bitter)
1 onion, roughly chopped
1 leek, roughly sliced
2 celery sticks, chopped

1 bay leaf
4 parsley stalks
$\frac{1}{2}$ tsp black peppercorns
$\frac{1}{2}$ tsp salt
1.3 l (2 $\frac{1}{4}$ pts) water

Makes about 1.2 l (2 pts)

Put the fish bones in a saucepan, and add all the remaining ingredients. Bring to the boil, then reduce the heat and simmer gently, skimming off any scum occasionally, for about 30 minutes. Strain the stock through a strainer and leave to cool completely, then chill or freeze it until ready to use.

serving soup

There are hundreds of different ways to serve soup, including when and how to present it. Soup can be served on its own, simply ladled into a bowl, or accompaniments, garnishes and toppings can be added to transform a plain soup into something extraordinary. Even if you don't have the time to make a saucepan of soup, you can transform a bowl of ready-made soup; try some of the following suggestions.

accompaniments

Chunks, wedges or slices of bread are probably the simplest of all accompaniments. There is plenty of choice, including bought or home-made.

Lightly bake a loaf of bread, ready to heat it in the oven while the soup cooks. This is a clever choice as it gives the impression that the bread is freshly baked with none of the effort of making a loaf at the same time as making soup.

Try different types of bread, include crusty baguettes and wholegrain loaves; Italian ciabatta and flavoured focaccia; wholesome rye breads (such as pumpernickel) and individual rolls. More unusual choices include savoury scones, wedges of warm naan bread or pitta bread. You may want to serve the bread plain or with butter for spreading.

Bread can be plain or toasted. Small slices of toasted bread, such as baguette, ciabatta or brioche can be topped to make bruschetta or crostini. These delicious accompaniments can be served on the side or floated on top of the soup as a sophisticated garnish. Garlic bread is another great accompaniment that can be made simply by splitting a baguette or ciabatta, spreading the slices with garlic butter, wrapping in foil and heating in the oven until hot and crisp.

A cheeseboard, perhaps with a small selection of cheese and some grapes or celery, is an excellent choice for complementing the soup and bread, making a delicious light, but satisfying, meal.

garnishes

One of the joys of serving soup is the wide choice of garnishes that can be added so easily just before serving. From a sprinkling of herbs, a swirl of cream to crispy croûtons, tangy salsas, crispy shallots or even a couple of ice cubes for a chilled soup. Whatever you choose, with a little care, it can transform a simple bowl of soup into a gourmet treat. Garnishes should add flavour, texture and the visual appeal that is so important for whetting the appetite and stimulating the taste buds.

croûtons

These crispy cubes of toasted or fried bread are a classic topping for soups, bringing crunchy texture contrast. The simplest croûtons are made from cubes of bread, fried in olive oil or butter until crisp, then drained on kitchen paper and left to cool. You can make big chunky croûtons out of thick slices. Throw a little crushed garlic into the saucepan about 1 minute before the end of cooking time. Cubes or wedges of toasted naan bread, ciabatta or focaccia also make good croûton-type toppings for soup.

bruschetta & crostini

Slices of baguette or ciabatta, brushed with oil, then grilled until crisp and golden, are perfect with soup, either as a chunky garnish or an accompaniment instead of bread. For hearty soups, they are a good alternative to little croûtons – make them plain, or rub one side with a cut clove of garlic. Drizzle with more oil and sprinkle with herbs and ground black pepper, or top with seeded, chopped tomatoes or a spoonful or two of salsa. Another option is to spread them with pesto and top with chargrilled vegetables; or add a dollop of soured cream or mayonnaise on to bite-size crostini and top with a twist of smoked salmon or salami. The options are endless, so let your imagination run riot.

vegetable crisps

Great for serving on the side, a handful of potato or vegetable crisps are a simple alternative to crispy croûtons. Try sweet potato, beetroot and carrot crisps for colour and sweet flavour. Experiment with traditional types, very thin crisps and thick-cut types. Just scatter a handful on top of the soup seconds before serving.

fresh herbs

For colour, flavour and aroma, fresh herbs are an easy and delicious choice when it comes to finishing soups. Snipped chives or a sprinkling of chopped parsley, mint or sage look and taste fabulous. Fine cutting is important for firm-textured herbs, but soft leaves can be left whole or torn. Some herbs are best when finely shredded – sage leaves, for example, can be rolled and cut into very fine shreds. Torn basil leaves, or whole leaves or sprigs of herbs, such as thyme or oregano, all look lovely sprinkled over soup just before serving. Herb flowers are a great choice when in season and they look especially pretty on delicate, special-occasion soups or pale-coloured cream soups.

chilli

Spicy soups look lively when garnished with sliced, diced or slivered chillies, but be sure to seed them and remove the white pith inside as this is where the heat resides.

spring onions

Fresh spring onions, very thinly sliced or shredded, look good and they add fresh colour and punchy flavour. They are traditional and excellent with Asian-style soups and broths, but also work well sprinkled on a wide variety of other soups, such as simple tomato soup, for extra taste and texture.

onion rings

Wafer thin slices of raw onion, divided into rings can look appetising and they bring a twist of flavour to the more subtle soups. Red onions are a good choice for their colour and mild flavour; white onions or Spanish onions are also delicious.

salad vegetables

Finely diced cucumber, peppers and tomatoes make good-looking garnishes, particularly on summer soups. Just use one, or toss a few different vegetables together with herbs and a drizzle of olive oil, red wine vinegar and seasoning, then spoon on top of the soup.

citrus fruits

Grated lemon, orange or lime rind look fresh and add a particularly distinctive, zesty flavour that cannot be achieved by using juice alone. Finely grated citrus rind is also delicious sprinkled on simple bruschetta after grilling.

seeds

Toasted seeds, such as sesame, pumpkin and sunflower, go well with soup. Not only do they look appetising and add a wonderful texture and colour, they are also a healthy option. Try them in place of croûtons and combine them with finely chopped herbs.

ice cubes

Perfect for finishing chilled soups, a few cubes of ice bobbing in a bowl add a certain sophistication, keeping the soup chilled on a hot day. Add them seconds before serving.

toppings

Toppings are perfect for spooning, swirling, or floating. Cream, yoghurt, flavoured oils, dressings or relishes are all suitable – experiment with textures and flavours to complement the soup they are dressing. When selecting a topping, think about the main ingredients, how substantial they are, and whether they would benefit from being enriched or from a complementary refreshing topping.

Yoghurt

Yoghurt makes a low-fat alternative to cream and works particularly well spooned or swirled on top of Indian-style spiced soups. For swirling or drizzling, select thin yoghurt or thin down the thicker types, such as strained Greek-style yoghurt, by stirring in a little milk.

cream

Pale cream contrasts with richly coloured soup. Creams are particularly good for topping smooth, blended soups. Single or double cream can be drizzled or swirled into soup just before serving; heavier creams, such as crème fraîche and soured cream, are added in dollops. Cream enriches the flavour of the soup, at the same time taking the edge off punchy ingredients – making them more mellow.

pesto

Richly flavoured pesto looks good and adds flavour. It works particularly well with Mediterranean-style soups and vegetable soups. It can be used plain or blended with a little extra-virgin olive oil for finer drizzling. Homemade classic pesto, with fresh basil, garlic, pine nuts, Parmesan cheese and olive oil, bursts with flavour and bright green colour. When selecting shop-bought pesto, go for a good-quality product. There are many variations on the traditional classic paste, including pesto with peppers, tomatoes, herbs other than basil, different nuts and various oils.

salsas, relishes & chutneys

These can be spooned on top of soups to give an extra zing. Make your own, or buy good-quality products. These can be chunky or fairly smooth, piquant, mild or hot and spicy. Instead of spooning them straight on the soup, try topping toasted finely sliced bread or slightly larger croûtons.

fish, ham & bacon

Strips of smoked salmon or flakes of smoked fish can make a stunning finishing touch scattered on the surface of soup just before serving. A small spoonful of caviar, perhaps paired with a dollop of soured cream, looks and tastes terrific. Wafer-thin strips of Parma ham or prosciutto can be used in the same way. For a crispy topping, try grilling a couple of rashers of bacon until crisp, then snip them into pieces and scatter these over the soup, rather like croûtons.

cheese

Try scattering grated cheese on top of a hearty vegetable soup, or top with shavings of Parmesan cheese. Crumbly cheeses, such as Stilton or feta, are also perfect for sprinkling. Creamy cheeses, such as gorgonzola or goat's cheese, can be cut into small cubes and scattered on top. The cheese melts with the heat of soup, producing a lovely texture and enriching the flavour.

pancakes & omelettes

Fine pancakes and thin omelettes are perfect for topping broths or lightly thickened soups. They should be well flavoured and finely cut, either by rolling, slicing and shaking out into thin shreds, or cut into small shapes using cocktail cutters. Neatly diced omelette, cut into strips and then across, is also good on soup. Herbs, spices and/or finely chopped vegetables, such as spring onions, peppers and tomatoes, are good cooked in the omelette or pancake.

cooled & chilled

When it's hot and sunny outside, nothing quite
beats a bowl of lusciously flavoured, ice-cold soup.
Chilled soups make the perfect choice for a simple
yet sophisticated appetiser too – so serve one up
before a special dinner.

iced carrot & orange soup

see variations page 38

This fresh, zesty soup makes a delicious appetiser, or refreshingly light summer lunch or supper, served with chunks of crusty bread.

2 tbsp olive oil
1 onion, chopped
450 g (1 lb) carrots, sliced
1 small potato, chopped

1.2 l (2 pts) vegetable stock
Juice of 2 oranges
Salt and ground black pepper
Ice cubes and chopped fresh mint, to garnish

Heat the oil in a saucepan. Add the onion and cook gently for about 5 minutes. Stir in the carrots and potato, and pour in the stock. Bring to the boil, then reduce the heat and cover the pan. Simmer for about 20 minutes, until the vegetables are tender.

Purée the soup in a blender until smooth. Pour the soup into a bowl, cover and leave to cool. Stir in the orange juice and chill the soup for at least 2 hours.

Check the seasoning, adding salt and pepper to taste, and ladle the soup in bowls. Add a couple of ice cubes to each bowl of soup and sprinkle with fresh mint.

Serves 4

chilled avocado soup with fiery tomato salsa

see variations page 39

Smooth, creamy and incredibly quick to make, this luscious soup is perfect for a quick lunch or supper.

2 large, ripe avocados
1 red chilli, seeded and chopped
1 garlic clove, chopped
1.2 l (2 pts) chicken stock, chilled
Juice of 1 lime
Salt and ground black pepper
Ice cubes, to serve

for the salsa

2 ripe tomatoes, seeded and finely chopped
2 spring onions, sliced
1 green chilli, seeded and finely chopped
2 tbsp chopped fresh coriander
Juice of ½ lime

First make the salsa. Combine the tomatoes, spring onions, chilli and coriander in a small bowl. Season with a little salt, squeeze the lime juice over the mixture and stir until combined. Cover and set aside.

To make the soup, halve and stone the avocados, then scoop the flesh into a food processor or blender. Add the chilli, garlic and stock, and process until smooth. Add the lime juice and season to taste with salt and pepper, then process briefly to mix.

Pour the soup into bowls. Top with ice cubes and a spoonful of salsa. Serve immediately.

Serves 4

vichyssoise

see variations page 40

This classic chilled soup is perfect for an al fresco lunch on a hot summer's day or as an elegant appetiser before a special meal.

25 g (1 oz) butter
3 leeks, sliced
1 medium-large potato, chopped
800 ml (28 fl oz) vegetable stock

350 ml (12 fl oz) milk, plus extra to finish
150 ml (¼ pt) single cream
Salt and ground black pepper
Snipped chives and croûtons, to garnish

Melt the butter in a large saucepan. Add the leeks, stir and cook gently for about 5 minutes, until softened. Add the potato and stock and bring to the boil. Reduce the heat, cover and simmer for about 15 minutes, until the potato is tender.

Process the soup in a food processor or blender until smooth. Stir in the milk and cream and season to taste with salt and pepper. Leave to cool, then chill for at least 2 hours.

To serve, taste and add more salt and pepper if necessary. Add a splash more milk if the soup is slightly too thick, then ladle it into bowls. Sprinkle each portion with chives and croûtons, and serve immediately.

Serves 4

simple spanish gazpacho

see variations page 41

The secret to getting a really good flavour when making this classic Spanish soup is to use good-quality, ripe ingredients, particularly the tomatoes.

900 g (2 lb) ripe tomatoes, peeled, seeded and
    roughly chopped
1 cucumber, peeled and roughly chopped
1 red pepper, seeded and roughly chopped
1 red onion, roughly chopped
2 garlic cloves, crushed
5 tbsp olive oil
About 350 ml (12 fl oz) cold water

3 slices dry (stale) bread, crusts removed and
    cut into chunks
2 tbsp sherry vinegar
Pinch of sugar
Salt and ground black pepper
Finely diced red onion, cucumber and fresh basil
    leaves, to garnish

Put the tomatoes, cucumber, pepper, onion and garlic in a food processor. Add the olive oil. Pour in about half the water and place the bread on top. Process until thick and smooth.

Transfer the soup to a large bowl. Stir in most of the remaining water, vinegar, sugar and salt and pepper to taste. Chill for at least 2 hours.

To serve, check the consistency and add a splash more water if necessary. Ladle the soup into bowls. Garnish with onion, cucumber and a few basil leaves, and serve.

Serves 4

cucumber & yoghurt soup

see variations page 42

Popular in the Middle East, this simple, quick and refreshing soup is perfect in summer, either as an appetiser or a light lunch.

3 cucumbers, seeded and roughly chopped
350 ml (12 fl oz) Greek yoghurt
250 ml (8 fl oz) vegetable stock, chilled
2 tbsp chopped fresh mint, plus extra to garnish

Salt and ground black pepper
Paprika, for sprinkling
4 spring onions, cut into short lengths and
    finely shredded

Purée the cucumbers in a food processor or blender until smooth. Add the yoghurt and stock and pulse briefly to combine.

Pour the soup into a large bowl. Stir in the mint and add salt and pepper to taste, then chill for at least 2 hours or until ready to serve.

Ladle the soup into bowls. Sprinkle each portion with mint, a pinch of paprika and spring onions, and serve

Serves 4

chilled tomato & basil soup with tomato sorbet

see variations page 43

This light, elegant soup makes a stylish appetiser before a special meal. It is particularly good in summer, when tomatoes are ripe and basil plentiful.

2 tbsp olive oil
1 onion, chopped
2 garlic cloves, crushed
1 kg (1 lb 2 oz) tomatoes, peeled and chopped
½ tsp soft brown sugar
1.2 l (2 pts) vegetable or chicken stock
Handful of fresh basil
Salt and ground black pepper

for the sorbet

500 g (1 lb 2 oz) tomatoes, peeled and seeded
¼ red chilli, seeded and chopped
½ garlic clove, crushed
1 tsp soft brown sugar
¼ tsp balsamic vinegar
Handful of fresh basil, plus extra to garnish

For the sorbet, purée the tomatoes, chilli, garlic, sugar, vinegar and basil in a food processor. Add salt and pepper to taste and chill. Churn in an ice cream-maker or freeze in a suitable container (3 to 8 hours), processing twice in a food processor to break up the ice crystals.

Heat the oil in a saucepan. Add the onion and garlic, and cook gently for 5 minutes. Add the tomatoes, sugar and stock. Bring to the boil, then simmer, covered, for 20 minutes. Cool, blend until smooth, adding the basil, and chill for at least 2 hours. Place a scoop of sorbet in each bowl. Ladle in the soup, garnish with a few fresh basil leaves and serve immediately.

Serves 4

sweet pea & mint soup

see variations page 44

This lovely, fresh, green soup is incredibly simple and takes less than 15 minutes to make.

2 tbsp olive oil
4 shallots, chopped
2 garlic cloves, crushed
1 kg (2¼ lb) frozen peas

1.2 l (2 pts) vegetable or chicken stock
1 tbsp chopped fresh mint, plus extra to garnish
Salt and ground black pepper
120 ml (4 fl oz) double cream

Heat the oil in a large saucepan. Add the shallots and garlic, and cook gently for about 2 minutes. Stir in the peas and vegetable stock. Bring to the boil, then remove from the heat.

Process the soup in a blender or food processor until smooth. Stir in the mint and salt and pepper to taste. Leave the soup to cool and then chill it for at least 2 hours before serving.

Check the consistency of the soup and stir in a splash of water if necessary. Pour the soup into bowls or glasses. Swirl in the cream and serve sprinkled with more fresh mint.

Serves 4

chilled sorrel soup

see variations page 45

Fresh sorrel comes into season in spring. It has an intense and sharp, lemon-like flavour.

1 small potato, diced
900 ml (1½ pts) vegetable stock
Bunch of spring onions, shredded
450 g (1 lb) sorrel, roughly shredded

175 ml (6 fl oz) white wine
120 ml (4 fl oz) double cream
Salt and ground black pepper
Snipped chives, to garnish

Put the potato and stock in a large saucepan. Bring to the boil, reduce the heat, cover and simmer for about 15 minutes, until the potato is tender.

Stir in the spring onions and three-quarters of the sorrel. Process the soup in a food processor or blender until smooth. Pour the soup into a large bowl. Stir in the wine, cream, remaining sorrel and salt and pepper to taste. Leave the soup to cool, then chill it for at least 2 hours before serving.

Ladle the soup into bowls and sprinkle with snipped chives, then serve immediately.

Serves 4

beetroot & orange soup with sour cream

see variations page 46

This sweet, fragrant, ruby red soup makes a stunning starter. It is refreshing for a summer lunch or uplifting at any time of the year.

2 tbsp olive oil
1 onion, chopped
750 g (1 lb 10 oz) raw beetroot, peeled and
    chopped
1.2 l (2 pts) vegetable or chicken stock
½ tsp grated orange rind

Juice of 2 oranges
Salt and ground black pepper
1½ tbsp sour cream
4 cocktail blinis
Snipped fresh chives and grated orange rind,
    for sprinkling

Heat the oil in a large saucepan. Add the onion and cook gently for about 5 minutes. Add the beetroot and stock, stir and bring to the boil. Reduce the heat, cover and simmer for about 20 minutes, until the beetroot is tender.

Process the soup in a food processor or blender until smooth. Pour into a large bowl and leave to cool. Stir in the orange rind, juice and salt and pepper to taste. Chill the soup for at least 2 hours.

To serve, spoon a small dollop of soured cream on each blini and sprinkle with orange rind and chives. Ladle the soup into serving bowls and float a blini on each portion.

Serves 4

lettuce & spring onion soup

see variations page 47

This light and simple soup makes a refreshing appetiser on a hot day.

2 tbsp olive oil
1 onion, chopped
2 garlic cloves, crushed
1 l (1¾ pts) vegetable or chicken stock
4 baby gem lettuces, shredded
2 bunches spring onions, sliced

120 ml (4 fl oz) dry white wine
3 tbsp mayonnaise
½ tsp harissa
4 slices baguette
Chopped fresh parsley, for sprinkling
Salt and ground black pepper

Heat the oil in a large saucepan. Add the onion and garlic, and cook gently for 5 minutes. Pour in the stock and bring to the boil. Stir in the lettuce and spring onions, and cook for about 1 minute, then remove from the heat.

Process the soup in a food processor or blender until smooth. Pour the soup into a large bowl. Stir in the wine. Add salt and pepper to taste. Leave the soup to cool, then chill it for at least 2 hours.

To serve, combine the mayonnaise and harissa. Toast the baguette slices on both sides until golden and top with mayonnaise and a sprinkling of parsley. Ladle the soup into serving bowls and float a toast on each portion. Serve immediately.

Serves 4

variations

iced carrot & orange soup

see base recipe page 19

iced carrot, tomato & orange soup
Prepare the basic recipe, adding 3 peeled, chopped tomatoes with
the carrots.

iced carrot, pepper & orange soup
Prepare the basic recipe, adding 2 seeded, chopped red peppers with
the carrots.

creamy iced carrot & orange soup
Prepare the basic recipe, stirring 3 tablespoons mascarpone into the blended
soup before cooling and chilling. Serve topped with a swirl of cream.

iced carrot, orange & coriander soup
Prepare the basic recipe, stirring 2 tablespoons chopped fresh coriander into
the cooled soup. Serve sprinkled with more coriander in place of the mint.

iced carrot, leek & orange soup
Prepare the basic recipe, using 1 sliced leek in place of the onion.

chilled avocado soup with fiery tomato salsa

see base recipe page 21

chilled avocado soup with fiery tomato salsa toasts
Prepare the basic recipe and pour the soup into bowls, but do not top with salsa. Toast 8 slices of baguette on both sides until golden, then top with the salsa and drizzle with a little olive oil. Serve immediately, with the soup, garnished with ice cubes.

chilled avocado soup with fiery tomato salsa & soured cream
Prepare the basic recipe. Serve the soup topped with a dollop of soured cream as well as the salsa and ice.

chilled avocado soup with fiery tomato salsa & crunchy tortillas
Prepare the basic recipe. Do not add ice cubes but top each bowl of soup with tortilla chips. Serve the salsa separately with more tortilla chips.

hot avocado soup with fiery tomato salsa
Prepare the basic recipe. Pour the soup into a saucepan and heat it gently until almost simmering. Serve in bowls, topped with the salsa but omitting the ice cubes.

variations

vichyssoise

see base recipe page 22

vichyssoise with garlic & chive toasts
Prepare the basic recipe. Blend 50 g (2 oz) butter with 1 crushed garlic clove,
2 tablespoons snipped chives and a good grinding of black pepper. Toast
8 slices of baguette on both sides until golden, then spread with the butter
and serve with the soup.

extra-creamy vichyssoise
Prepare the basic recipe and serve each bowl topped with a generous swirl
of cream before adding the chives and croûtons.

vichyssoise with fresh mint
Prepare the basic recipe and serve sprinkled with chopped fresh mint in
place of the chives.

leek & potato soup
Prepare the basic recipe. Return the puréed soup to the rinsed-out saucepan
and stir in the milk and cream. Reheat, stirring often, until almost boiling.
Ladle into bowls, sprinkle with chives and croûtons, and serve.

variations

simple spanish gazpacho

see base recipe page 25

simple spanish gazpacho with crispy croûtons
Prepare the basic recipe. Cut 3 slices of crustless bread into cubes. Fry in about 2 tablespoons olive oil until golden. Drain on paper towels and sprinkle over the soup. (Omit the onion, cucumber and basil garnish, if preferred.)

classic gazpacho
Prepare the basic recipe, omitting the garnish. Prepare croûtons as in the above variation. Finely dice 1 small red onion, 1 green pepper and 1 small cucumber. Sprinkle the diced vegetables and croûtons over the soup.

fragrant simple spanish gazpacho
Prepare the basic recipe, adding a handful of basil leaves before blending.

simple spanish gazpacho with garlic toasts
Prepare the basic recipe. Toast 4 to 8 slices of rustic sourdough bread. Rub with a cut clove of garlic, then drizzle with olive oil. Serve with the soup.

simple spanish gazpacho with chorizo
Prepare the basic recipe. Fry slices of thinly sliced chorizo in a little olive oil until crisp, then serve sprinkled over the soup with or without the basic garnish.

variations

cucumber & yoghurt soup

see base recipe page 26

cucumber & yoghurt soup with pitta toasts
Prepare the basic recipe. To serve, toast 2 pitta breads, then split them in half and cut into wedges. Place, toasted sides down, on the grill pan and sprinkle with a little chopped garlic and a drizzle of olive oil. Grill until golden. Sprinkle with chopped fresh parsley and serve with the soup.

cucumber & yoghurt soup with herbs
Prepare the basic recipe, reducing the mint to 1 tablespoon and adding 1 tablespoon snipped fresh chives and 1 tablespoon chopped fresh parsley. Sprinkle with more chopped fresh herbs before serving.

cucumber & yoghurt soup with red pepper
Prepare the basic recipe. Seed and finely dice 1 small cucumber and 1 red pepper and sprinkle over the soup with the spring onions and mint.

cucumber & yoghurt soup with lemon
Prepare the basic recipe, adding the grated rind of 1 lemon with the yoghurt and stock.

chilled tomato & basil soup with tomato sorbet

see base recipe page 29

convenient chilled tomato & basil soup with tomato sorbet
Prepare the basic recipe using canned tomatoes in place of fresh.

cream of tomato & basil soup
Prepare the basic soup recipe, but not the sorbet. Return the blended soup
to the saucepan and stir in 120 ml (4 fl oz) double cream. Heat through
without boiling and serve topped with a swirl of cream.

chilled tomato & mint soup with tomato sorbet
Prepare the basic recipe, using mint in place of the basil.

chilled tomato & herb soup with tomato sorbet
Prepare the basic recipe, stirring in 2 tablespoons snipped fresh chives,
1 tablespoon chopped fresh mint and 1 tablespoon chopped fresh parsley
into the chilled soup.

variations

sweet pea & mint soup

see base recipe page 30

sweet pea & mint soup with prosciutto
Prepare the basic recipe. Sprinkle each bowl of soup with bite-size strips of prosciutto ham before serving.

sweet pea & mint soup with crispy bacon
Prepare the basic recipe. Grill 2–3 bacon rindless bacon rashers until crisp, then cut them into bite-size pieces. Sprinkle over the soup to serve.

sweet pea & mint soup with smoked salmon
Prepare the basic recipe. Sprinkle each bowl of soup with strips of smoked salmon to serve.

piping hot sweet pea & mint soup
Prepare the basic recipe and purée it freshly cooked. Reheat briefly if necessary, but do not overcook, and serve swirled with cream.

low-fat sweet pea & mint soup
Prepare the basic recipe, omitting the cream.

variations

chilled sorrel soup

see base recipe page 33

chilled sorrel & spinach soup
Prepare the basic recipe, adding 115 g (4 oz) baby spinach leaves with the first batch of sorrel.

iced sorrel soup
Float a few ice cubes in each bowl of soup before serving.

chilled spring leaf soup
Prepare the basic recipe, adding a handful of baby spinach leaves and a handful of rocket leaves with the sorrel.

chilled sorrel & chive soup
Prepare the basic recipe. Stir in 2 tablespoons snipped fresh chives before chilling. Serve sprinkled with more chives.

variations

beetroot & orange soup with soured cream

see base recipe page 34

chunky beetroot & orange soup with soured cream
Prepare the basic recipe, using finely chopped beetroot. Process half the
cooked soup, then return it to the saucepan. Stir in the orange rind and
juice, and serve hot, topped with the blini.

beetroot & orange soup with vodka & soured cream
Prepare the basic recipe, stirring in 4 tablespoons vodka just before serving.

quick beetroot & orange soup with soured cream
Prepare the basic recipe, using cooked beetroot in place of raw. Fry the
onion, then add the beetroot and chilled stock. Blend without simmering.

spiced beetroot & orange soup with soured cream
Prepare the basic recipe, adding 2 teaspoons ground coriander to the onion
before stirring in the beetroot and stock.

variations

lettuce & spring onion soup

see base recipe page 37

lettuce, pea & spring onion soup
Prepare the basic recipe, adding 250 g (9 oz) frozen peas with the stock.

lettuce, asparagus & spring onion soup
Prepare the basic recipe, adding 250 g (9 oz) trimmed, sliced asparagus with the stock. Simmer the soup for about 3 minutes before adding the lettuce and spring onions.

lettuce, spinach & spring onion soup
Prepare the basic recipe, adding 2 large handfuls of spinach with the lettuce.

lettuce & spring onion soup with lemon
Prepare the basic recipe. Stir 1 teaspoon grated lemon rind into the cooled soup before serving.

healthy &
wholesome

Soup is a great choice when you're looking for

a meal that will sustain and nourish. Low in fat

and packed with fresh, nutritious ingredients and

slow-release carbs, the soups in this chapter are all

designed to give your body the health kick it needs.

chicken noodle soup

see variations page 68

This comforting, wholesome, home-made soup is an old-fashioned cure-all – ideal when you're nursing a cold, or just to lift your spirits.

2 chicken leg portions (about 500 g /
   1 lb 2 oz), skinned
1 onion, quartered
3 celery sticks, sliced
1 large carrot, sliced
1 bay leaf

Small bunch of fresh parsley, plus handful of
   flat-leaf parsley leaves to serve
1.5 l (2¾ pts) water
Salt and ground black pepper
115 g (4 oz) angel hair noodles or vermicelli

Put the chicken, onion, celery, carrot, bay leaf and bunch of parsley in a large saucepan. Pour in the cold water. Add about ¾ teaspoon salt and a good grinding of black pepper and bring to the boil. Reduce the heat, cover and simmer for about 20 minutes, or until the chicken is cooked.

Remove the chicken, strip off the meat and set it aside. Return the bones to the saucepan. Cover and simmer for a further 1½ hours. Meanwhile, cut the chicken into small pieces.

Strain the stock into a clean saucepan and bring it back to the boil. Break the noodles into pieces, add them to the stock and simmer for 5 minutes, until tender. Stir in the chicken and heat it through. Stir in the parsley leaves and serve.

Serves 4

spiced lentil, chickpea & chorizo soup

see variations page 69

This chunky, wholesome soup is packed with fibre and complex carbohydrates offering slow-release energy to keep you going for longer.

100 g (3½ oz) Puy lentils
2 tbsp olive oil
55 g (2 oz) chorizo, chopped
1 onion, finely chopped
2 garlic cloves, crushed
3 tsp ground cumin
2 tsp ground coriander
½ tsp ground cinnamon

¼ tsp crushed dried chilli
4 tomatoes, peeled, seeded and chopped
400 g (14 oz) can chickpeas, rinsed and drained
1 tbsp tomato purée
1.2 l (2 pts) vegetable or chicken stock
Salt and ground black pepper
Juice of about ½ lemon, to taste

Put the lentils in a large saucepan, pour in enough boiling water to cover them generously and simmer for about 20 minutes, until just tender. Drain well.

Heat the oil in the rinsed-out pan and gently fry the chorizo, onion and garlic for 4 minutes. Stir in the cumin, coriander, cinnamon and chilli, followed by the tomatoes, chickpeas, tomato purée and stock. Bring to the boil, reduce the heat, cover and simmer for 15 minutes.

Add salt and pepper and lemon juice to taste. Ladle the soup into bowls and serve.

Serves 4

carrot, leek & potato soup

see variations page 70

This thick, warming soup is fat-free (depending on the stock used) so it makes a filling, yet healthy, meal for those following a low-fat diet.

3 carrots, roughly chopped
2 leeks, sliced
1 small potato, roughly chopped
1.2 l (2 pts) vegetable or chicken stock

Salt and ground black pepper
Chopped fresh flat-leaf parsley, to garnish
Crusty wholegrain bread, to serve

Put the carrots, leeks and potatoes in a large saucepan. Pour in the stock and bring to the boil. Reduce the heat and simmer for about 20 minutes, until the vegetables are tender.

Process the soup in a food processor or blender until smooth. Add salt and pepper to taste, then pour the soup into serving bowls. Sprinkle with parsley and serve with chunks of crusty wholegrain bread.

Serves 4

sweet-and-sour red cabbage soup with bacon

see variations page 71

This richly coloured, robust sweet-and-sour soup makes a perfect winter warmer. Serve with thick slices of crusty bread and a mature Cheddar cheese.

1 tbsp olive oil
3 rindless streaky bacon rashers, snipped into
    bite-size pieces
2 onions, finely chopped
300 g (10½ oz) red cabbage, shredded
1 apple, peeled, cored and finely chopped
2 tbsp cider vinegar

2 tbsp soft brown sugar
4 juniper berries, crushed
2 cloves
¼ tsp grated nutmeg
1.2 l (2 pts) vegetable stock
Salt and ground black pepper

Heat the oil in a large saucepan. Add the bacon and onions, and cook gently for 5 minutes.

Add the cabbage, apple, vinegar, sugar, juniper berries, cloves and nutmeg. Pour in the stock and stir well. Bring to the boil, reduce the heat and cover the saucepan. Simmer the soup for about 20 minutes, until the cabbage is tender.

Add salt and pepper to taste before serving the soup.

Serves 4

ribollita

see variations page 72

This classic Italian soup is hearty and substantial. It is full of fibre and the vegetable goodness of cabbage, tomatoes and beans.

2 tbsp olive oil
1 onion, finely chopped
2 garlic cloves, crushed
400-g (14-oz) can chopped tomatoes
1 tbsp tomato purée

1.2 l (2 pts) vegetable or chicken stock
400-g (14-oz) can flageolet beans, drained
   and rinsed
225 g (8 oz) Savoy cabbage, shredded
Salt and ground black pepper

Heat the oil in a large saucepan. Add the onion and garlic, and cook gently for about 4 minutes. Add the tomatoes, tomato purée, stock and beans. Stir well, then bring to the boil. Reduce the heat and simmer gently for about 20 minutes.

Transfer about half the beans and vegetables to a food processor and add a couple of ladlefuls of the stock. Process to a smooth purée, then stir the purée back into the soup.

Add the cabbage, bring back to the boil and reduce the heat. Simmer for 5 to 10 minutes, until the cabbage is tender. Add salt and pepper to taste and serve.

Serves 4

green bean soup with tuna & tapenade toasts

see variations page 73

This chunky vegetable soup, packed with green beans, is inspired by the classic Niçoise salad. Any leftover tapenade can be stored in the fridge for another use.

2 tbsp olive oil, plus extra for brushing
1 onion, finely chopped
2 garlic cloves, crushed
4 ripe tomatoes, peeled and chopped
1 l (1¾ pts) vegetable stock
1 large potato, finely diced
225 g (8 oz) green beans, cut into
   3-cm (1¼-in) lengths
Salt and ground black pepper
115 g (4 oz) tuna steak

4 slices baguette
1 hard-boiled egg, quartered

for the tapenade

100 g (3½ oz) stoned black olives
1 garlic clove, crushed
2 anchovy fillets
1 tsp capers, rinsed and drained
2 tbsp olive oil

Heat the oil in a large saucepan and cook the onion and garlic for 5 minutes. Add the tomatoes and stock. Boil, reduce the heat, cover and simmer for 10 minutes. Add the potato and cook for 5 minutes, then the beans and cook for 3 minutes. Add salt and pepper to taste. For the tapenade, purée all the ingredients in a food processor. Season with pepper. Brush the tuna on both sides with oil and season with salt and pepper. Heat a non-stick frying pan, sear the tuna for 1 to 2 minutes on each side, then slice into thick strips. Toast the baguette, spread with tapenade, top with tuna and egg. Ladle the soup into bowls and add the toasts.

Serves 4

black bean soup with soured cream

see variations page 74

This thick, nourishing soup makes a healthy lunch or supper dish.

300 g (10½ oz) dried black beans, soaked
　　overnight in cold water
2 tbsp olive oil
1 onion, chopped
3 garlic cloves, crushed
¼ tsp crushed dried chilli

2 tsp ground cumin
1 tsp ground coriander
1.2 l (2 pts) vegetable or chicken stock
Juice of 2 limes, or to taste
Salt and ground black pepper
5 tbsp soured cream
Chopped fresh coriander, to garnish

Drain the beans and put in a large saucepan. Pour in boiling water to cover generously and boil rapidly for 10 minutes, skimming off any scum that rises to the surface. Reduce the heat, cover and simmer for about 1 hour, until the beans are tender. Drain.

Heat the oil in the rinsed-out saucepan. Add the onion and garlic, and cook gently for about 5 minutes. Stir in the chillies, cumin and coriander, followed by the beans and stock. Bring to the boil. Reduce the heat, cover and simmer gently for about 10 minutes. Process the soup in a food processor or blender until smooth. Stir in lime juice and salt and pepper to taste. Ladle the soup into bowls, top with soured cream and garnish with coriander.

Serves 4

beef & barley soup

see variations page 75

This chunky broth offers everything you need in a meal – protein, carbohydrate and fresh vegetables cooked until just tender.

2 tbsp olive oil
450 g (1 lb) lean tender steak, cubed
1 onion, finely chopped
2 garlic cloves, crushed
115 g (4 oz) pearl barley
1.3 l (2¼ pts) beef stock

1 tsp fresh thyme leaves
3 carrots, chopped
3 celery sticks, sliced
1 large potato, diced
Salt and ground black pepper

Heat the oil in a large non-stick saucepan. Add the beef and cook quickly until browned all over. Use a slotted spoon to transfer the meat to a plate and set aside. Add the onion and garlic to the saucepan, and fry gently for about 4 minutes, then add the barley, stock and thyme. Replace the beef.

Bring to the boil, reduce the heat, cover and simmer for about 45 minutes. Add the carrots, celery and potato, and simmer for a further 15 minutes, until the meat and vegetables are tender. Season the soup to taste, then ladle it into bowls and serve.

Serves 4

mediterranean vegetable soup

see variations page 76

This rich tomato broth is spiked with capers to make a wonderfully healthy, light soup for summer and early autumn, when these vegetables are at their best.

2 tbsp olive oil
1 onion, finely chopped
2 garlic cloves, crushed
4 large ripe tomatoes, peeled and chopped
1 red pepper, seeded and finely chopped
1 tbsp sun-dried tomato purée

1.2 l (2 pts) vegetable or chicken stock
2 courgettes, quartered and sliced
4 tsp capers, rinsed and chopped
Handful of fresh basil leaves, torn
Salt and ground black pepper

Heat the oil in a large saucepan. Add the onion and garlic, and cook gently for 5 minutes. Add the tomatoes, pepper, tomato purée and stock, and bring to the boil. Reduce the heat, cover and simmer for 10 minutes.

Add the courgettes and capers, and simmer for a further 10 minutes, until tender. Stir in the basil leaves and salt and pepper to taste. Ladle the soup into bowls and serve.

Serves 4

chunky root vegetable soup

see variations page 77

This satisfying soup is packed with vegetables to make a nutritious, filling lunch or supper.

2 tbsp olive oil
1 onion, finely chopped
1 garlic clove, crushed
3 carrots
200 g (7 oz) celeriac, peeled and cubed
3 small turnips, peeled and cubed

400-g (14-oz) can chopped tomatoes
1 tbsp tomato purée
1.2 l (2 pts) vegetable or chicken stock
1 tsp. fresh oregano leaves
Salt and ground black pepper

Heat the oil in a large saucepan. Add the onion and garlic, and cook gently for 5 minutes. Add the carrots, celeriac, turnips, tomatoes, tomato purée, stock and oregano. Stir well and bring to the boil.

Reduce the heat, cover the saucepan and simmer the soup for about 20 minutes, until the vegetables are tender. Add salt and pepper to taste before serving the soup.

Serves 4

variations

chicken noodle soup

see base recipe page 49

creamy chicken noodle soup
Prepare the basic recipe and stir in 120 ml (4 fl oz) double cream just before serving.

chicken noodle soup with spring onions
Prepare the basic recipe, adding 1 bunch sliced spring onions about 1 minute before the end of cooking time.

chicken noodle soup with chorizo
Prepare the basic recipe, adding 55 g (2 oz) chopped chorizo to the broth with the chicken meat.

hot & spicy chicken noodle soup
Prepare the basic recipe, adding 2 chopped, seeded red chillies with the other vegetables.

chicken noodle soup with apricots
Prepare the basic recipe, adding 85 g (3 oz) chopped ready-to-eat dried apricots to the strained broth. Simmer for 15 minutes before adding the noodles and continue as in the main recipe.

spiced lentil, chickpea & chorizo soup

see base recipe page 51

vegetarian spiced lentil & chickpea soup
Prepare the basic recipe, using vegetable stock and omitting the chorizo.

spiced lentil, flageolet bean & chorizo soup
Prepare the basic recipe, using flageolet beans in place of the chickpeas.

thick spiced lentil, chickpea & chorizo soup
Prepare the basic recipe. Before seasoning and adding lemon juice, ladle half the soup into a food processor or blender and blend until smooth. Return the smooth soup to the saucepan and heat gently. Season and add lemon juice to taste, then serve.

spiced lentil, chickpea & chorizo soup with spicy harissa
Prepare the basic recipe, adding 1 teaspoon harissa paste to the soup with the other spices.

spiced lentil, chickpea & chorizo soup with fresh coriander
Prepare the basic recipe. Sprinkle chopped fresh coriander into the soup before serving.

variations

carrot, leek & potato soup

see base recipe page 52

carrot, leek & potato soup with mustard
Prepare the basic recipe, stirring 1 tablespoon wholegrain mustard into the soup before adding salt and pepper.

carrot, leek & potato soup with cheese
Prepare the basic recipe, ladle into bowls and serve sprinkled with grated Cheddar cheese.

carrot, leek & beetroot soup
Prepare the basic recipe, using 1 peeled and diced cooked beetroot in place of the potato.

carrot, leek, potato & tomato soup
Prepare the basic recipe, then add a 400-g (14-oz) can chopped tomatoes with the other vegetables.

carrot, leek & potato soup with mustard and cheese
Prepare the basic recipe, adding 1 tablespoon wholegrain mustard when puréeing the soup, and sprinkle with grated cheese before serving.

sweet-and-sour red cabbage soup with bacon

see base recipe page 55

vegetarian sweet-and-sour red cabbage soup
Prepare the basic recipe, omitting the bacon.

sweet-and-sour red cabbage & beetroot soup with bacon
Prepare the basic recipe, adding 1 raw or cooked beetroot, peeled and cut into matchstick strips, with the cabbage.

fruity sweet-and-sour red cabbage soup with bacon
Prepare the basic recipe, adding a handful of sultanas with the cabbage.

spiced sweet-and-sour red cabbage soup with bacon
Prepare the basic recipe, adding 1 teaspoon crushed cumin seeds and 1 teaspoon ground coriander with the other spices.

sweet-and-sour red cabbage soup with bacon and chickpeas
Prepare the basic recipe, adding a 400-g (14-oz) can rinsed, drained chickpeas to the saucepan with the cabbage.

variations

ribollita

see base recipe page 56

classic ribollita
Prepare the basic recipe, using shredded cavolo nero cabbage in place of the Savoy cabbage.

mixed bean ribollita
Prepare the basic recipe, using a 400-g (14-oz) can mixed beans in place of the flageolet beans.

spicy ribollita
Prepare the basic recipe, adding ½ teaspoon crushed dried chilli with the tomatoes.

rustic ciabatta ribollita
Prepare the basic recipe. Tear half a ciabatta loaf into chunks and add them to the soup just before ladling it into bowls.

rich vegetable ribollita
Prepare the basic recipe, adding 2 chopped carrots and 4 chopped celery sticks with the tomatoes.

variations

green bean soup with tuna & tapenade toasts

see base recipe page 59

veggie green bean soup with egg & tapenade toasts
Prepare the basic recipe, but omit the anchovies from the tapenade and omit
the tuna. Top each toast with a quarter of a hard-boiled egg.

broad bean soup with tuna & tapenade toasts
Prepare the basic recipe, using shelled, fresh broad beans instead of green
beans.

runner bean soup with tuna & tapenade toasts
Prepare the basic recipe, using sliced runner beans in place of green beans.

simple green bean soup
Prepare the basic recipe, omitting the tapenade and tuna toasts, and serve
with chunks of crusty bread.

variations

black bean & soured cream soup

see base recipe page 60

red kidney bean soup with soured cream
Prepare the basic soup, using kidney beans in place of the black beans.

black bean soup with soured cream & parsley
Prepare the basic recipe, scattering the bowls of soup with chopped fresh parsley in place of the coriander.

black-eyed bean soup with soured cream
Prepare the basic recipe, using black-eyed beans in place of the black beans.

black bean soup with tomatoes, soured cream & salsa
Prepare the basic recipe, adding a 400-g (14-oz) can chopped tomatoes with the stock. Serve topped with soured cream and a spoonful of tomato salsa.

black bean soup with tortilla chips, soured cream & spring onions
Prepare the basic recipe. Serve topped with tortilla chips, soured cream and shredded spring onions.

variations

beef & barley soup

see base recipe page 63

lamb & barley soup
Prepare the basic recipe, using cubed lamb in place of the beef.

chicken & barley soup
Prepare the basic recipe, using 3 cubed, skinless chicken breasts in place of
beef, and chicken stock in place of the beef stock. Add the chicken with the
vegetables, rather than with the barley.

beef & barley soup with tomatoes
Prepare the basic recipe, adding a 400-g (14-oz) can chopped tomatoes with
the barley.

beef & barley soup with oregano
Prepare the basic recipe, using fresh oregano in place of the thyme. Sprinkle
with fresh oregano leaves before serving.

variations

mediterranean vegetable soup

see base recipe page 64

mediterranean vegetable soup with pesto
Prepare the basic recipe, and drizzle each serving with a little pesto.

mediterranean vegetable soup with pasta
Prepare the basic recipe, adding a good handful of soup pasta to the saucepan with the courgettes.

mediterranean vegetable soup with parmesan
Prepare the basic recipe. Serve the soup sprinkled with shavings of Parmesan cheese.

mediterranean vegetable soup with pesto bruschetta
Prepare the basic recipe. Toast 8 slices of baguette until golden on both sides, then spread with pesto and top with a drained chargrilled artichoke in olive oil. Serve the bruschetta with the soup.

mediterranean vegetable soup with green beans
Prepare the basic recipe, adding 150 g (5 oz) trimmed, sliced green beans with the courgettes.

variations

chunky root vegetable soup

see base recipe page 67

smooth root vegetable soup
Prepare the basic recipe. Blend the soup until smooth in a food processor or blender before serving. Add a little more stock if the soup is too thick.

chunky root vegetable soup with bacon
Prepare the basic recipe, adding 3 roughly chopped, rindless bacon rashers with the onion and garlic.

chunky beetroot & mixed vegetable soup
Prepare the basic recipe, using 1 large, peeled and diced, raw beetroot in place of the turnips.

chunky root vegetable soup with black-eyed beans
Prepare the basic recipe, adding a 400-g (14-oz) can drained, rinsed black-eyed beans with the vegetables.

smooth & creamy

A big pan of rich, creamy soup offers ultimate comfort in its simplest form. Mild and moreish, rich and flavoursome or hot and spicy, there's something for everyone in this chapter.

fennel soup with blue cheese

see variations page 98

With a subtle aniseed flavour cut by the sharp tang of blue cheese, this smooth creamy soup makes an utterly luxurious feast, served with chunks of crusty bread.

25 g (1 oz) butter
2 onions, chopped
3 bulbs of fennel with fronds
1 potato, chopped

1 l (1¾ pts) vegetable stock
200 ml (7 fl oz) single cream
75 g (2½ oz) blue cheese, crumbled
Salt and ground black pepper

Melt the butter in a large saucepan. Add the onions and cook gently for about 4 minutes. Meanwhile, trim the fennel fronds from the bulbs and reserve them, then slice the bulbs and add to the pan with the potato and stock. Bring to the boil. Reduce the heat, cover and simmer for about 20 minutes, until the vegetables are tender.

Process the soup in a food processor or blender until smooth. Return the soup to the pan. Stir in the cream, about three-quarters of the cheese and salt and pepper to taste.

Warm through, then ladle the soup into bowls. Sprinkle over the remaining cheese and fennel fronds and serve.

Serves 4

wild mushroom soup with sage

see variations page 99

Make this soup in autumn, when wild mushrooms are in season and plentiful.

25 g (1 oz) butter
1 onion, chopped
2 garlic cloves, crushed
1 tbsp plain flour
1 l (1¾ pts) vegetable or chicken stock
750 g (1 lb 10 oz) wild mushrooms, chopped

6 fresh sage leaves, chopped
120 ml (4 fl oz) white wine
120 ml (4 fl oz) double cream
Salt and ground black pepper
Chopped fresh parsley, to garnish

Melt the butter in a large saucepan. Add the onion and garlic, and cook for about 4 minutes, until softened. Stir in the flour and cook for 1 minute more, then gradually stir in the stock. Add the mushrooms and bring to the boil. Reduce the heat, cover and simmer gently for about 15 minutes, until the mushrooms are tender. Stir in the sage.

Remove a couple of ladlefuls of the mushrooms and set aside. Process the remaining soup in a food processor or blender until smooth. Return the soup to the saucepan, add the reserved mushrooms and stir in the wine, cream and salt and pepper to taste. Warm through, without boiling. Ladle into bowls and sprinkle with parsley to garnish.

Serves 4

almond & garlic soup with fresh grapes

see variations page 100

This classic Spanish soup is very rich and therefore served in small portions – making it perfect as an appetiser.

115 g (4 oz) blanched almonds
2 garlic cloves, crushed
85 g (3 oz) fresh white breadcrumbs
570 ml (1 pt) cold vegetable stock

1 tbsp sherry vinegar
Ground black pepper
200 g (7 oz) green grapes, peeled and halved
Ice cubes, to serve (optional)

Heat a non-stick frying pan. Add the almonds and stir over low heat for about 3 minutes, until toasted. Tip into a food processor or blender and process to a fine powder. Add the garlic, breadcrumbs and about a quarter of the stock, then process to a smooth paste. Gradually add the rest of the stock, blending to a smooth soup.

Pour the soup into a bowl. Stir in the vinegar and pepper to taste. Chill for at least 2 hours. To serve, check the seasoning, adding more pepper if required, then ladle the soup into bowls. Add a few ice cubes to each portion (if using), and sprinkle the grapes over the top.

Serves 4

spinach & coconut soup

see variations page 101

Rich with coconut milk and fragrant with spices, this intriguing soup makes a great alternative to most classic cream soups, and is great for those on a dairy-free diet.

2 tbsp sunflower oil
1 onion, chopped
2 garlic cloves, crushed
2 green chillies, seeded and chopped
2 tsp ground cumin
1 tsp ground coriander
½ tsp turmeric

½ tsp ground ginger
570 ml (1 pt) vegetable stock
570 ml (1 pt) coconut milk
500 g (1 lb 2 oz) spinach
Juice of ½ lemon, to taste
Salt
Coconut shavings, toasted, to garnish (optional)

Heat the oil in a large saucepan. Add the onion, garlic and chillies, and cook gently for about 4 minutes. Stir in the cumin, coriander, turmeric and ginger, then add the stock and coconut milk and bring to the boil. Reduce the heat, cover the saucepan and simmer the soup for about 10 minutes.

Stir in the spinach and cook for about 2 minutes, until the leaves wilt. Process about three-quarters of the soup in a food processor or blender until smooth. Return the smooth soup to the saucepan, stir in lemon juice and salt to taste. Heat gently for a few seconds, if necessary, then ladle into serving bowls. Sprinkle with coconut shavings, if liked, and serve.

Serves 4

roast pepper & mascarpone soup

see variations page 102

Sweet, smooth and creamy, with a deliciously rich and slight smoky flavour, this soup is excellent in summer and early autumn, when sweet peppers and tomatoes are perfect.

6 red peppers
2 tbsp olive oil
1 onion, chopped
2 garlic cloves, crushed
3 ripe tomatoes, peeled and chopped

1.2 l (2 pts) vegetable stock
6 tbsp mascarpone cheese
Handful of fresh basil leaves, plus extra
    to garnish
Salt and ground black pepper

Preheat the oven to 230°C (450°F / Gas 8). Arrange the peppers on a baking sheet and cook for 30 minutes, until charred. Transfer the peppers to a bowl, cover with cling film and leave to stand for 15 minutes, until cool enough to handle.

Heat the oil in a large saucepan, then cook the onion and garlic for 4 minutes. Add the tomatoes and stock. Boil, reduce the heat, cover and simmer for 10 minutes.

Peel the peppers, remove the seeds and put the flesh in a food processor or blender with any juices. Add the mascarpone. Pour in the soup, add the basil and process until smooth. Season with salt and pepper to taste and serve sprinkled with fresh basil leaves.

Serves 4

creamy courgette & dill soup

see variations page 103

Smooth, mild and creamy, and gently flavoured with aromatic dill, this soup tastes wonderfully luxurious without being too rich.

2 tbsp olive oil
1 onion, chopped
2 garlic cloves, crushed
1.2 kg (2 lb 12 oz) courgettes, sliced
1 l (1¾ pts) vegetable or chicken stock

1½ tbsp dried or fresh dill, plus extra fresh dill
   to garnish
120 ml (4 fl oz) single cream
Salt and ground black pepper
Juice of about ¼ lemon, to taste

Heat the oil in a large saucepan. Add the onion and garlic, and cook for about 5 minutes. Stir in the courgettes and stock, and bring to the boil. Reduce the heat, cover and simmer gently for 5 to10 minutes, until the courgettes are tender.

Add the dill, then process the soup in a food processor or blender until smooth. Add the cream and salt and pepper to taste, and pulse to mix. Add a squeeze of lemon juice to taste, then ladle into bowls and serve garnished with dill.

Serves 4

cream of wine & mussel soup

see variations page 104

This sophisticated soup is perfect as an appetiser and just as good for a light meal, served with chunks of crusty white bread.

1.5 kg (3 lb 5 oz) mussels, cleaned
40 g (1½ oz) butter
3 garlic cloves, crushed
300 ml (½ pt) white wine

750 ml (1¼ pts) fish stock
150 ml (¼ pt) double cream
2 tbsp chopped fresh parsley
Salt and ground black pepper

Discard any open mussels that do not close when tapped sharply. Heat the butter in a large saucepan and fry the garlic for 1 minute. Add the mussels, pour over half the wine, cover the saucepan tightly and cook over high heat for about 4 minutes, to steam the mussels until their shells are open.

Drain the mussels through a colander or fine sieve placed over a clean saucepan. Stand the colander over a bowl and put to one side. Add the remaining wine and stock to the strained liquor and heat gently until simmering.

Discard any shells that have not opened. Shell about two-thirds of the mussels and add them to the soup. Warm through for a few seconds, then remove the saucepan from the heat. Stir in the cream and parsley, with salt and pepper to taste. Ladle the soup into bowls and garnish with the remaining mussels in their shells.

Serves 4

cream of onion soup with chives

see variations page 105

This thick and rich soup is perfect on a cold, dark evening, when you need a little warming, comfort food.

2 tbsp olive oil
1 kg (2 lb 4 oz) Spanish onions, chopped
1 small potato, diced
1.2 l (2 pts) vegetable or chicken stock
180 ml (6 fl oz) single cream

2 tbsp snipped fresh chives, plus extra to garnish
Salt and ground black pepper
Breadsticks, to serve

Heat the oil in a large saucepan. Add the onions and cook gently for about 20 minutes, until soft and translucent. Add the potato and stir in the stock. Bring the soup to the boil. Reduce the heat, cover and simmer for about 10 minutes, until the potato is tender.

Process the soup in a food processor or blender until smooth. Return the soup to the rinsed-out saucepan. Stir in the cream, chives and salt and pepper to taste. Reheat without boiling.

Ladle the soup into serving bowls and sprinkle with more chives. Serve immediately, while piping hot, with breadsticks.

Serves 4

watercress soup

see variations page 106

This light, creamy soup is the perfect way to cook peppery watercress. Serve it as an appetiser, or a light meal with big chunks of crusty bread.

25 g (1 oz) butter
1 onion, chopped
1 potato, chopped
750 ml (1¼ pts) vegetable or chicken stock

225 g (8 oz) watercress
300 ml (½ pt) milk
4 tbsp double cream
Salt and ground black pepper

Melt the butter in a large saucepan. Add the onion and cook gently for 4 minutes. Add the potato and stir in the stock. Bring to the boil. Reduce the heat, cover and simmer gently for about 15 minutes, or until the potato is tender.

Meanwhile, gently pull the leaves off the watercress and shred the stalks. Add the stalks to the soup and simmer for about 1 minute, then add three-quarters of the leaves and simmer for 1 minute more.

Process the soup in a food processor or blender until smooth. Return the soup to the rinsed-out saucepan, stir in the milk and cream, and warm through without boiling. Reserve a few of the remaining watercress leaves for garnish, then stir the rest into the soup, with salt and pepper to taste. Serve sprinkled with the last of the watercress.

Serves 4

potato & garlic soup

see variations page 107

Velvety smooth and full of fragrant garlic, this simple soup is homely and comforting.

2 tbsp olive oil
1 onion, chopped
6 garlic cloves, crushed
2 large potatoes, chopped
800 ml (28 fl oz) chicken stock

400 ml (14 fl oz) milk
Juice of about ½ lemon, to taste
Salt and ground black pepper
4 tbsp single cream
2 tbsp chopped fresh parsley

Heat the oil in a large saucepan. Add the onion and garlic, and cook gently for about 4 minutes. Stir in the potatoes and stock, and bring to the boil. Reduce the heat, cover and simmer for about 15 minutes, until the potatoes are tender.

Process the soup in a food processor or blender until smooth. Return the soup to the rinsed-out saucepan, add the milk and heat through without boiling. Stir in lemon juice and salt and pepper to taste.

To serve, ladle the soup into bowls, drizzle a tablespoon of cream into each bowl, add a grinding of black pepper and sprinkle with parsley.

Serves 4

variations

fennel soup with blue cheese

see base recipe page 79

celeriac soup with blue cheese & chives
Prepare the basic recipe, using 450 g (1 lb) celeriac in place of the fennel
and potato, and sprinkle with chives to garnish.

fennel soup with goat's cheese
Prepare the basic recipe, using 100 g (3½ oz) cubed goat's cheese in place of
the blue cheese

fennel soup with blue cheese & pear croûtes
Prepare the basic recipe, allowing extra blue cheese. Toast 4 slices of
baguette until golden on both sides. Top each with a slice of blue cheese and
a wedge of ripe pear. Float on top of the soup and serve.

fennel soup with goat's cheese toasts
Prepare the basic recipe, omitting the blue cheese. Toast four slices of
walnut bread on one side. Turn over, spread with goat's cheese and grill until
melting, then serve with the soup.

fennel & celery soup with blue cheese
Prepare the basic recipe, using 2 fennel bulbs and 6 sliced celery sticks.

variations

wild mushroom soup with sage

see base recipe page 81

wild mushroom soup with thyme
Prepare the basic recipe, adding 1 teaspoon fresh thyme leaves with the stock and omitting the sage.

cheat's wild mushroom soup with sage
Prepare the basic recipe, using cultivated mushrooms instead of wild ones. Soak 15 g (½ oz) dried porcini in a little boiling water for 20 minutes, then add to the soup, including the soaking water, with the stock.

wild mushroom soup with garlic toasts
Prepare the basic recipe. Beat 60 g (2 oz) soft butter with 2 crushed garlic cloves and season with black pepper. Toast 8 slices of baguette, spread with the garlic butter and serve with the soup.

wild mushroom & chicken soup with sage
Prepare the basic recipe. Shred 2 skinless cooked chicken breasts, stir into the soup and warm through before serving.

wild mushroom soup with sage & crispy bacon
Prepare the basic recipe. To serve, grill 3 rindless bacon rashers until crisp, then snip them into bite-size pieces and sprinkle over the soup.

almond & garlic soup with fresh grapes

see base recipe page 82

hazelnut & garlic soup with fresh grapes
Prepare the basic soup, using blanched hazelnuts in place of the almonds.

almond & garlic soup with garlic toasts
Prepare the basic recipe. To serve, toast 8 slices baguette on both sides until golden. Rub one side of each with a cut garlic clove and drizzle with extra-virgin olive oil. Serve with the soup instead of the grapes.

almond & garlic soup with grapes & fresh mint
Prepare the basic recipe, sprinkling each serving with chopped fresh mint.

almond & garlic soup with grapes & fresh parsley
Prepare the basic recipe, sprinkling each serving with chopped fresh parsley.

almond & garlic soup with grapes & spring onions
Prepare the basic recipe. Thinly slice 2 spring onions and sprinkle over the soup with the grapes.

variations

spinach & coconut soup

see base recipe page 85

curried spinach & coconut soup
Prepare the basic recipe, using 2 tablespoons curry paste in place of
the dry spices.

thai-style spinach & coconut soup
Prepare the basic recipe, using 2 tablespoons green curry paste in place
of the cumin, coriander and turmeric.

broccoli & coconut soup
Prepare the basic recipe, using broccoli in place of the spinach. Cut
the broccoli into florets and cook for about 10 minutes, until tender,
before blending.

cream of spinach soup
Prepare the basic recipe, using 1 litre (1¾ pts) vegetable stock and omitting
the chilli, dried spices and coconut milk. Stir in 120 ml (4 fl oz) single cream
just before serving and season with salt, pepper and freshly grated nutmeg
to taste.

variations

roast pepper & mascarpone soup

see base recipe page 86

chilled roast pepper & mascarpone soup
Prepare the basic recipe and leave the soup to cool. Chill for at least 2 hours and serve sprinkled with fresh basil leaves.

roast pepper & crème fraîche soup
Prepare the basic recipe, using crème fraîche in place of mascarpone. Serve topped with a dollop of crème fraîche and fresh basil leaves.

roast pepper & mascarpone soup with chives
Prepare the basic recipe, omitting the basil. Stir 2 tablespoons snipped chives into the blended soup, and serve sprinkled with more chives.

roast mixed pepper & mascarpone soup
Prepare the basic recipe, using a mixture of red, orange and yellow peppers.

spicy roast pepper & mascarpone soup
Prepare the basic recipe, adding 2 seeded, chopped red chillies with the onion and garlic.

variations

creamy courgette & dill soup

see base recipe page 89

marrow & dill soup
Prepare the basic recipe, using peeled, seeded marrow in place of the courgettes.

creamy courgette & chive soup
Prepare the basic recipe, omitting the dill. Stir 2 tablespoons snipped chives into the blended soup, and serve sprinkled with more snipped chives.

creamy courgette, spinach & dill soup
Prepare the basic recipe, adding 3 large handfuls of spinach leaves about 2 minutes before the end of cooking time. Blend and season as before.

creamy courgette, broccoli & dill soup
Prepare the basic recipe, using 500 g (1 lb 2 oz) courgettes and adding 500 g (1 lb 2 oz) broccoli, cut into bite-size florets.

chilled creamy courgette & dill soup
Prepare the basic recipe, then leave the soup to cool and chill for at least 2 hours before serving.

variations

cream of wine & mussel soup

see base recipe page 90

creamy mussel soup with vermouth
Prepare the basic recipe, using vermouth in place of the white wine.

cream of wine & mussel soup with chives
Prepare the basic recipe, using snipped chives in place of the parsley.

cream of cider & mussel soup
Prepare the basic recipe, using cider in place of the white wine.

cream of wine & mussel soup with shallots
Prepare the basic recipe, using 3 finely chopped shallots and reducing the garlic to 1 crushed clove.

cream of wine & crab soup
Prepare the basic recipe, omitting the mussels. Stir in two 170-g (6-oz) cans white crabmeat with the stock.

variations

cream of onion soup with chives

see base recipe page 93

cream of onion soup with white wine & chives
Prepare the basic recipe, using 1 l (1¾ pts) stock and 200 ml (7 fl oz) white wine.

cream of onion soup with thyme
Prepare the basic recipe, adding 1 teaspoon fresh thyme leaves with the stock and omitting the chives.

cream of onion soup with chives & garlic croûtes
Prepare the basic recipe. To serve, slice a small baguette diagonally. Toast the slices on both sides until golden, then spread with garlic butter and serve with the soup.

cream of onion soup with spring onions
Prepare the basic recipe, sprinkling the soup with sliced spring onions instead of chives.

variations

watercress soup

see base recipe page 94

chilled watercress soup
Prepare the basic recipe, then leave to cool and chill for at least 2 hours before serving.

watercress & spring onion soup
Prepare the basic recipe, adding 1 bunch sliced spring onions with the watercress.

dairy-free watercress soup
Prepare the basic recipe, using soya milk in place of dairy milk. (Be careful not to boil the soup or it will curdle.)

watercress & spinach soup
Prepare the basic recipe, adding 2 handfuls of spinach leaves with the watercress.

variations

potato & garlic soup

see base recipe page 97

potato & garlic soup with sage
Prepare the basic recipe, using 2 teaspoons chopped fresh sage in place of
the parsley.

potato, leek & garlic soup
Prepare the basic recipe, using 1 sliced leek in place of the onion.

potato, carrot & garlic soup
Prepare the basic recipe, using 1 potato and 3 sliced carrots.

potato & garlic soup with potato crisps
Prepare the basic recipe. Serve the soup topped with a handful of lightly
crushed potato crisps.

potato & garlic soup with crispy bacon
Prepare the basic recipe. To serve, grill 4 rindless bacon rashers until crisp,
then snip them into pieces over the bowls of soup.

meal in a bowl

Hearty, nutritious, wholesome soup makes a
wonderful feast in a single bowl. Whichever
delicious soup you choose from this chapter,
it's sure to be more than enough to keep you
going until your next meal.

chunky seafood soup

see variations page 128

There are countless stew-like fish soups, such as French bouillabaise, that make the most of the catch of the day: this chunky broth takes its inspiration from those classic origins.

2 tbsp olive oil
1 onion, finely chopped
3 garlic cloves, crushed
400-g (14-oz) can tomatoes
800 ml (28 fl oz) fish stock
¼ tsp crushed dried chilli
1 tsp fresh thyme leaves

750 g (1 lb 10 oz) mussels, cleaned
450 g (1 lb) firm white fish, cut into
    bite-size chunks
200 g (7 oz) raw prawns, shelled and deveined
2 tbsp chopped fresh parsley
Salt and ground black pepper
Crusty bread, to serve

Heat the oil in a large saucepan. Add the onion and garlic, and cook for 4 minutes. Add the tomatoes, stock, chilli and thyme. Boil, reduce the heat, cover and simmer for 20 minutes.

Discard any open mussels that do not close when tapped sharply. Bring 4 tablespoons water to the boil in a large saucepan. Add the mussels, cover tightly and cook for about 5 minutes, until the shells open. Drain the mussels, discarding any unopened shells. Shell about three-quarters of the mussels, then set all of them aside.

Add the fish and prawns to the soup and simmer for 2–3 minutes, until the fish is cooked through and the prawns are pink. Add all the mussels and heat through for a few seconds. Add salt and pepper to taste, sprinkle with the parsley and serve with chunks of bread.

Serves 4

chilli beef soup with cheese-topped tortilla chips

see variations page 129

This hearty soup makes a warming meal for all the family. Serve with more tortilla chips or chunks of crusty bread on the side.

2 tbsp olive oil
1 onion, finely chopped
2 garlic cloves, crushed
3 red chillies, seeded and chopped
250 g (9 oz) minced beef
2 tsp ground cumin
400-g (14-oz) can chopped tomatoes
1 tsp sun-dried tomato paste

1 green pepper, seeded and chopped
400-g (14-oz) can kidney beans, rinsed and
    drained
800 ml (28 fl oz) beef stock
½ tsp fresh thyme leaves
Salt and ground black pepper
2 handfuls tortilla chips
Cheddar cheese, grated, for sprinkling

Heat the oil in a large saucepan. Add the onion, garlic and chillies, and cook gently for about 4 minutes. Add the beef and fry for about 5 minutes, stirring often, until browned all over. Stir in the cumin, tomatoes, sun-dried tomato paste, stock and thyme, and bring to the boil. Reduce the heat, cover and simmer for about 15 minutes.

Add the pepper and beans to the soup and simmer for a further 10 minutes. Stir in salt and pepper to taste. Ladle the soup into bowls and top each portion with tortilla chips and a sprinkling of cheese. Serve immediately.

Serves 4

moroccan-style lamb soup with couscous

see variations page 130

This meaty soup is a contemporary take on the traditional Morrocan tagine, cooked with lamb, spices and dried apricots.

3 tbsp olive oil
1 onion, finely chopped
2 garlic cloves, crushed
350 g (12 oz) lean lamb, cubed
¼ tsp cayenne pepper
1 tsp paprika
1 tsp ground cumin
1 tsp ground coriander

2 tsp ground cinnamon
400-g (14-oz) can chopped tomatoes
1.5 l (2¾ pts) lamb or beef stock
115 g (4 oz) ready-to-eat dried apricots, halved
140 g (5 oz) couscous
175 ml (6 fl oz) boiling water
Salt and ground black pepper
2 tbsp chopped fresh mint

Heat 2 tbsp of the oil in a large saucepan. Add the onion and garlic and cook gently for 4 minutes. Stir in the lamb, cayenne, paprika, cumin, coriander, cinnamon, tomatoes, stock and apricots. Boil, reduce the heat, cover and simmer for 1½ hours, until the lamb is tender.

Put the couscous in a medium bowl, season with salt and use a fork to mix in the remaining oil. Pour in the water and leave to soak for 5 minutes. Fluff up the couscous, stir in most of the mint, and divide it among four bowls, mounding it in the middle of each. Add salt and pepper to the soup, then ladle it around the couscous. Sprinkle with the remaining mint.

Serves 4

smoked haddock & mange tout chowder

see variations page 131

Salty smoked haddock and tender mange tout make a great combination in this hearty, chunky fish broth.

2 tbsp olive oil
1 onion, finely chopped
475 ml (16 fl oz) fish stock
350 g (12 oz) smoked haddock
2 large potatoes, diced

700 ml (24 fl oz) milk
200 g (7 oz) mange tout, sliced
2 tbsp chopped fresh parsley
Salt and ground black pepper

Heat the oil in a large saucepan. Add the onion and cook gently for 5 minutes. Pour in the stock, add the haddock and heat until barely simmering. Poach for about 6 minutes, until the fish is cooked. Use a fish slice to remove the fish. Add the potatoes to the pan and bring to the boil. Reduce the heat, cover and simmer for 10 minutes, until the potatoes are tender.

Skin the haddock and break the flesh into large flakes, discarding any bones. Ladle half the soup into a food processor or blender and process until smooth, then return it to the pan. Add the milk and mange tout, and heat gently until almost simmering. Replace the fish and reheat for about 2 minutes, until the mange tout are just tender. Add the parsley, salt and pepper to taste, and serve.

Serves 4

pasta & meatball soup

see variations page 132

This chunky, hearty soup is great when you want a comforting and substantial meal.

250 g (9 oz) lean minced beef
½ onion, grated
2 garlic cloves, crushed
½ tsp dried oregano
1 tbsp grated Parmesan cheese, plus shavings
    to garnish
Salt and ground black pepper

1 tbsp olive oil
400-g (14-oz) can chopped tomatoes
750 ml (1¼ pts) beef stock
1 tbsp tomato purée
100 g (3½ oz) conchigliette or other small
    pasta shapes
Fresh oregano leaves, to garnish

Mix the beef, onion, half the garlic, half the oregano and the Parmesan, and season well with salt and pepper. Roll the mixture into about 20 bite-size meatballs.

Heat the oil in a large saucepan. Working in batches if necessary, add the meatballs and brown them all over. Transfer the meatballs to a plate when browned.

Add the remaining garlic to the pan and fry for 1 minute. Replace the meatballs and add the tomatoes, stock, tomato purée and remaining oregano. Add salt and pepper to taste and simmer gently for about 15 minutes.

Add the pasta shapes and simmer for a further 8 to 10 minutes, until tender. Taste the soup and add more salt and pepper, if necessary, then serve sprinkled with Parmesan and oregano.

Serves 4

spicy sausage & bean soup

see variations page 133

This soup makes a hearty treat and is particularly good after a cold winter walk. It can be made ahead and reheated before serving.

2 tbsp olive oil
5 good-quality pork sausages
1 onion, chopped
2 garlic cloves, finely chopped
1½ red chillies, seeded and chopped
400-g (14-oz) can chopped tomatoes

750 ml (1¼ pts) beef or chicken stock
Two 400-g (14-oz) cans borlotti beans, rinsed
   and drained
2 tbsp chopped fresh parsley
Salt and ground black pepper

Heat the oil in a large saucepan. Add the sausages, brown them all over and then remove. Add the onion, garlic and chilli to the pan and fry gently for 3 minutes.

Cut the sausages into thick slices and return them to the pan, adding the tomatoes and stock. Bring to the boil, then reduce the heat, cover and simmer gently for about 20 minutes.

Put half the beans in a food processor or blender and add a couple of ladlefuls of the soup stock. Process until smooth, then stir the purée into the soup with the remaining beans and simmer for a further 10 minutes. Add salt and pepper to taste, and stir in the parsley before serving the soup.

Serves 4

roast squash risotto soup with goat's cheese

see variations page 134

This wholesome soup — a liquid risotto — makes a wonderfully sustaining meal.

1 butternut squash, seeded, peeled and cut
    into chunks
3 tbsp olive oil
Salt and ground black pepper
1 onion, finely chopped
2 garlic cloves, chopped
200 g (7 oz) risotto rice

175 ml (6 fl oz) white wine
1.2 l (2 pts) vegetable or chicken stock
6 fresh sage leaves, chopped, plus extra
    to garnish
100 g (4 oz) goat's cheese, cut into
    bite-size pieces

Preheat the oven to 200°C (400°F / Gas 6). Put the squash in a large baking dish, drizzle with 1 tablespoon of the oil and add salt and pepper to taste. Toss to coat the squash thoroughly and roast for about 30 minutes, until tender.

Meanwhile, heat the remaining oil in a large saucepan. Add the onion and garlic and cook gently for 5 minutes. Add the rice and cook for 2 minutes, stirring, then pour in the wine and allow to bubble gently, stirring, until most of the wine has been absorbed. Stir in the stock and bring to the boil. Reduce the heat and simmer gently, stirring frequently, for about 20 minutes, until the rice is tender. Stir the sage and squash into the soup, with salt and pepper to taste. Ladle the soup into bowls, sprinkle with goat's cheese and garnish with sage.

Serves 4

vermicelli soup with clams

see variations page 135

This fragrant, zesty broth is packed with tender clams and filling pasta to make a fabulous meal. Serve chunks of crusty baguette to mop up the broth.

900 g (2 lb) clams, cleaned
2 tbsp olive oil
1 onion, finely chopped
2 garlic cloves, crushed
120 ml (4 fl oz) vermouth
400-g (14-oz) can chopped tomatoes

1.2 l (2 pts) fish stock
1 tsp finely grated orange rind
Juice of 2 oranges
200 g (7 oz) vermicelli
2 tbsp chopped fresh parsley
Salt and ground black pepper

Discard any open clams that do not close when tapped sharply. Heat the oil in a large saucepan. Add the onion and garlic, and cook gently for 5 minutes. Add the clams and vermouth, cover and cook over fairly high heat for about 4 minutes, until the clams have opened. Remove the clams using a slotted spoon and set aside. Add the tomatoes, stock, orange rind and juice. Bring to the boil. Reduce the heat, cover and simmer for 10 minutes.

Meanwhile, discard any clams that have not opened. Reserve about 12 clams in their shells and shell the rest of the clams.

Add the vermicelli to the soup and cook for about 2 minutes, until tender. Add the clams and warm through. Add the parsley and salt and pepper to taste. Serve the soup garnished with the reserved clams in their shells.

Serves 4

spicy chicken & sweet potato soup with coconut milk

see variations page 136

Spicy, creamy and fragrant with peppery ginger, this delicious soup is packed with chunks of chicken and sweet potato to make a real meal in a bowl.

2 tbsp sunflower oil
1 onion, finely chopped
3 garlic cloves, crushed
2 tsp grated fresh root ginger
2 green chillies, seeded and finely chopped
½ tsp ground turmeric
2 tsp ground cumin
1 tsp ground coriander

2 sweet potatoes, diced
2 skinless, boneless chicken breasts,
    cut into bite-size pieces
400-ml (14-oz) can coconut milk
800 ml (28 fl oz) chicken stock
Juice of about ½ lemon, to taste
Salt and ground black pepper
Chopped fresh coriander, to serve

Heat the oil in a large saucepan. Add the onion and cook gently for 3 minutes. Add the garlic, ginger and chillies, and fry for a further 2 minutes. Stir in the turmeric, cumin and coriander. Add the sweet potatoes, chicken, coconut milk and stock. Bring to the boil. Reduce the heat, cover and simmer for 15 minutes, until the chicken and potatoes are cooked.

Crush about half the sweet potato using the back of the spoon or a fork. Stir the soup to mix in the crushed potato. Squeeze in lemon juice and add salt and pepper to taste, then sprinkle with chopped fresh coriander before serving.

Serves 4

pork & chickpea soup with zesty orange

see variations page 137

Lightly spiced and fragrant with orange, this cross between broth and stew is perfect when you need something both filling and fabulous.

2 tbsp olive oil
1 onion, finely chopped
2 garlic cloves, crushed
250 g (9 oz) lean pork loin, trimmed
    and cut into bite-size pieces
2 tsp ground cumin
2 tsp ground coriander

Grated rind and juice of 1 orange
400-g (14-oz) can chopped tomatoes
800 ml (28 fl oz) pork or chicken stock
Salt and ground black pepper
400-g (14-oz) can chickpeas, rinsed and drained
2 tbsp chopped fresh parsley
Juice of ½ lemon, or to taste

Heat the oil in a large saucepan. Add the onion and garlic, and cook gently for 4 minutes. Add the pork, sprinkle with the cumin and coriander, and cook, stirring, for about 1 minute. Stir in the orange rind and juice, tomatoes, stock and salt and pepper. Bring to the boil, then reduce the heat. Cover the pan and simmer for about 20 minutes.

Stir in the chickpeas and simmer for a further 10 minutes, until the pork is tender. Add more salt and pepper, if necessary, then stir in the parsley and lemon juice to taste before serving.

Serves 4

variations

chunky seafood soup

see base recipe page 109

chunky fish & prawn soup
Prepare the basic recipe, using 900 g (2 lb) firm white fish and 400 g (14 oz) prawns, and omitting the mussels.

fragrant seafood soup
Prepare the basic recipe, omitting the thyme. Just before serving, stir in a big handful of chopped fresh coriander.

curried chunky seafood soup
Prepare the basic recipe, adding 2 tablespoons curry paste in place of the thyme. Serve sprinkled with chopped fresh mint.

chunky seafood soup with fresh mint
Prepare the basic recipe, omitting the thyme. Just before serving, stir in 2 teaspoons chopped fresh mint and serve sprinkled with more fresh mint.

chunky seafood soup with fresh coriander
Prepare the basic recipe, omitting the thyme. Serve sprinkled with a handful of chopped fresh coriander.

chilli beef soup with cheese-topped tortilla chips

see base recipe page 111

chilli lamb soup with cheese-topped tortilla chips
Prepare the basic recipe, using minced lamb in place of the beef.

chilli turkey soup with cheese-topped tortilla chips
Prepare the basic recipe, using minced turkey in place of the beef, and chicken stock in place of the beef stock.

chilli pork soup with cheese-topped tortilla chips
Prepare the basic recipe, using minced pork in place of the beef.

rich tomato & beef soup
Prepare the basic recipe, omitting the chilli. Add 1 tablespoon (instead of 1 teaspoon) sun-dried tomato paste and 6 shredded sun-dried tomatoes with the stock. Serve with or without the tortilla chips.

chilli beef soup with pasta
Prepare the basic recipe, adding 115 g (4 oz) pasta 5 minutes before the end of cooking. Simmer until tender, then serve, omitting the tortilla chips.

variations

moroccan-style lamb soup with couscous

see base recipe page 112

moroccan-style lamb & pepper soup with couscous
Prepare the basic recipe, adding 2 seeded, chopped red peppers with
the lamb.

moroccan-style chicken soup with couscous
Prepare the basic recipe, using 4 skinless, boneless chicken breasts, cut into
bite-size pieces, in place of lamb, and chicken stock. Cook for 30 minutes.

moroccan-style chickpea soup with couscous
Prepare the basic recipe, using two 400-g (14-oz) cans drained, rinsed
chickpeas in place of the lamb, and vegetable stock in place of the meat
stock. Cook the soup for 30 minutes instead of 1½ hours.

moroccan-style fish soup with couscous
Prepare the basic recipe, omitting the lamb and using fish stock. Cook the
soup for 30 minutes, then add 450 g (1 lb) firm white fish, cut into bite-size
pieces, and cook for a further 5 minutes, or until the fish is cooked.

moroccan-style lamb soup with prunes & couscous
Prepare the basic recipe, using ready-to-eat dried prunes in place of apricots.

variations

smoked haddock & mange tout chowder

see base recipe page 115

smoked haddock & mange tout chowder with bacon
Prepare the basic recipe, adding 3 roughly chopped rindless bacon rashers
with the onions.

smoked haddock & mange tout chowder with rice
Prepare the basic recipe. Meanwhile, cook 200 g (7 oz) long-grain rice in a
separate pan of boiling water and then drain well. Spoon the rice into bowls
and ladle the chowder over the top.

spiced smoked haddock & mange tout chowder
Prepare the basic recipe, cooking 1 seeded, chopped red chilli with
the onion.

smoked haddock, mange tout & green pepper chowder
Prepare the basic recipe, adding 1 seeded, diced green pepper with
the potatoes.

smoked haddock & pea chowder
Prepare the basic recipe, adding 150 g (5 oz) thawed frozen peas with the
milk and omitting the mange tout.

variations

pasta & meatball soup

see base recipe page 116

pasta & turkey meatball soup
Prepare the basic recipe, using minced turkey in place of the beef, and chicken stock in place of the beef stock.

pasta & meatball soup with beans
Prepare the basic recipe, adding a drained, rinsed 400-g (14-oz) can flageolet beans with the pasta.

pasta & pork meatball soup
Prepare the basic recipe, using minced pork in place of the minced beef.

veggie pasta & bean soup
Prepare the basic recipe, omitting the meat and grated Parmesan cheese. Use vegetable stock instead of beef stock. Fry the onion and garlic in the oil for 5 minutes, then add the oregano, tomatoes and other ingredients. Add two drained, rinsed 400-g (14-oz) cans flageolet beans in place of meatballs.

spicy sausage & bean soup

see base recipe page 119

veggie sausage soup
Prepare the basic recipe, using vegetarian sausages and vegetable stock.

spicy sausage & bean broth
Prepare the basic recipe, adding one 400-g (14-oz) can borlotti beans and simmering without puréeing any of the soup

not-so-spicy sausage soup
Prepare the basic recipe, omitting the chillies and adding 1 teaspoon paprika.

spicy sausage, bean & roast red pepper soup
Prepare the basic recipe, adding 3 sliced, bottled roast peppers with the whole borlotti beans.

variations

roast squash risotto soup with goat's cheese

see base recipe page 120

roast squash risotto soup with blue cheese
Prepare the basic recipe, using blue cheese in place of the goat's cheese.

roast squash risotto soup with capers & chives
Prepare the basic recipe, omitting the sage. Stir 2 tablespoons snipped fresh chives and 2 teaspoons chopped capers into the finished soup.

roast beetroot risotto soup with goat's cheese
Prepare the basic recipe, using 2 to 3 large raw beetroot in place of the butternut squash. Roast the beetroot for 10 to15 minutes longer.

roast squash risotto soup with thyme & goat's cheese
Prepare the basic recipe, using 1 teaspoon thyme leaves in place of sage.

variations

vermicelli soup with clams

see base recipe page 123

vermicelli soup with mussels
Prepare the basic recipe, using mussels in place of the clams.

vermicelli soup with fish
Prepare the basic recipe, using 350 g (12 oz) firm white fish in place of the clams. Poach the fish until just cooked in the vermouth, then flake into large chunks, discarding skin and bones, and add to the soup at the last minute to warm through.

vermicelli soup with chicken
Prepare the basic recipe, using 350 g (12 oz) cooked chicken in place of the clams. Cut the chicken into bite-size chunks and add to the soup at the last minute to warm through.

vermicelli soup with prawns
Prepare the basic recipe, omitting the clams. Add 350 g (12 oz) peeled, deveined raw prawns with the vermicelli and cook until the prawns are pink and the pasta tender.

variations

spicy chicken & sweet potato soup with coconut milk

see base recipe page 124

spicy chicken & potato soup with coconut milk
Prepare the basic recipe, using ordinary potatoes in place of sweet potatoes.

spicy chicken, sweet potato & spinach soup with coconut milk
Prepare the basic recipe, adding 2 large handfuls of baby spinach leaves (or shredded large leaves) about 2 minutes before the end of cooking time.

spicy chicken & pumpkin soup with coconut milk
Prepare the basic recipe, using pumpkin or squash in place of the sweet potato.

spicy prawn & sweet potato soup with coconut milk
Prepare the basic recipe, omitting the chicken. About 2 minutes before the end of the cooking time, add 300 g (10½ oz) shelled and deveined raw tiger prawns, and simmer until pink and cooked through.

spicy pork & sweet potato soup with coconut milk
Prepare the basic recipe, using 300 g (10½ oz) diced lean pork loin in place of the chicken.

variations

pork & chickpea soup with zesty orange

see base recipe page 127

chickpea & orange soup
Prepare the basic recipe, omitting the pork, and using vegetable stock.
Simmer for 20 minutes, then stir in two 400-g (14-oz) cans drained, rinsed
chickpeas and cook for 10 minutes more.

chicken & chickpea soup with zesty orange
Prepare the basic recipe, using 2 skinless, boneless chicken breasts, cut into
bite-size pieces, in place of the pork, and chicken stock.

lamb & chickpea soup with zesty orange
Prepare the basic recipe, using lean shoulder of lamb, cut into bite-size
pieces, in place of the pork, and lamb or beef stock.

pork & flageolet bean soup with zesty orange
Prepare the basic recipe, using flageolet beans in place of the chickpeas.

20-minute treats

When you're in a hurry, there's still time to whip

up a delicious saucepan of soup. So much better

than just heating up a shop-bought canful, the

wonderful selection of soups in this chapter

take barely any longer – with each one taking

20 minutes or less to prepare.

broccoli soup with parmesan toasts

see variations page 158

The easiest way to make Parmesan shavings is to pare off wafer-thin slices using a vegetable peeler.

2 tbsp olive oil
1 onion, finely chopped
2 tbsp plain flour
750 ml (1½ pts) vegetable or chicken stock
450 g (1 lb) broccoli, cut into small florets
350 ml (12 fl oz) milk
½ tsp freshly grated nutmeg

Salt and ground black pepper

for the toasts

25 g (1 oz) butter, at room temperature
50 g (1¾ oz) freshly grated Parmesan cheese
8 slices baguette
25 g (1 oz) Parmesan, cut into shavings

Heat the oil in a large saucepan. Add the onion and cook gently for about 4 minutes. Stir in the flour and cook for 1 minute, then gradually stir in the stock. Add the broccoli, bring to the boil, then reduce the heat and simmer for about 7 minutes, until the broccoli is tender.

Process the soup in a blender or food processor until smooth, then return it to the saucepan. Stir in the milk, nutmeg and salt and pepper to taste, and heat through. Meanwhile, make the toasts. Beat the butter with the grated Parmesan. Grill the slices of baguette on one side, then turn and spread with the butter. Top with Parmesan shavings, grill until golden and bubbling, and serve with the soup.

Serves 4

spiced chickpea & lemon soup

see variations page 159

This warming, fragrant soup is delicious at any time of year. Use a can of chopped tomatoes when fresh ones are out of season.

2 tbsp olive oil
1 onion, chopped
2 garlic cloves, crushed
2 tsp ground cumin
1 tsp ground cinnamon
¼ tsp ground ginger

Two 400-g (14-oz) cans chickpeas
450 g (1 lb) ripe tomatoes, peeled and chopped
1 l (1¾ pts) chicken or vegetable stock
2 tbsp chopped fresh parsley
Juice of about ½ lemon, to taste
Salt and ground black pepper

Heat the oil in a large saucepan. Add the onion and garlic, and cook gently for 4 minutes. Stir in the cumin, cinnamon and ginger, then add half the chickpeas, the tomatoes and most of the stock, reserving about 200 ml (7 fl oz). Bring to the boil, reduce the heat and simmer for about 5 minutes.

Meanwhile, process the remaining chickpeas and reserved stock to a smooth purée in a food processor or blender. Stir the purée into the soup. Stir in the parsley. Add salt and pepper, and lemon juice to taste, and serve.

Serves 4

crab & sweetcorn chowder

see variations page 160

This rich, spicy chowder may be incredibly simple and quick to make, but it tastes like a sophisticated treat.

2 tbsp sunflower oil
1 onion, finely chopped
1 garlic clove, crushed
1 red chilli, seeded and chopped
2 potatoes, diced
1 red pepper, seeded and finely diced

570 ml (1 pt) stock
570 ml (1 pt) milk
Two 170-g (6-oz) cans crabmeat, drained
350-g (12-oz) can sweetcorn, drained
Salt and ground black pepper
2 tbsp chopped fresh parsley

Heat the oil in a large saucepan. Add the onion, garlic and chilli, and cook gently for 4 minutes. Stir in the potatoes, pepper and stock, and bring to the boil. Reduce the heat, cover and simmer for about 5 minutes, until the potatoes are tender.

Process half the soup until smooth in a food processor or blender. Add the milk, crabmeat and sweetcorn to the saucepan and heat through. Then return the puréed soup to the saucepan. Add salt and pepper to taste. Stir in the parsley and serve.

Serves 4

cappelletti in brodo

see variations page 161

This classic Italian soup of stuffed pasta in broth is traditionally served on New Year's Day, but it's the perfect choice any time you need an almost-instant bowl of soup.

1.2 l (2 pts) chicken stock
115 g (4 oz) cappelleti
4 tbsp white wine

2 tbsp chopped fresh parsley
Salt and ground black pepper
Parmesan cheese shavings, to serve

Bring the stock to the boil in a large saucepan. Add the pasta and cook according to the packet instructions, until al dente, tender with a bit of bite (not soft).

Stir in the wine, parsley and salt and pepper to taste. Ladle the soup into bowls and serve sprinkled with Parmesan shavings.

Serves 4

fresh vegetable minestrone

see variations page 162

Simple, healthy minestrone makes a great lunch or supper. Vary the choice of vegetables, if you like, according to what is good and in season.

2 tbsp olive oil
1 onion, finely chopped
2 garlic cloves, crushed
1 carrot, quartered and sliced
1 courgette, quartered and sliced
100 g (3½ oz) green cabbage, shredded

4 ripe tomatoes, peeled and chopped
1 tbsp sun-dried tomato purée
1.2 l (2 pts) vegetable stock
100 g (3½ oz) angel's hair pasta or vermicelli, broken into short lengths
Salt and ground black pepper

Heat the oil in a large saucepan. Add the onion and garlic, and cook gently for 4 minutes. Add the carrot, courgette, cabbage, tomatoes, tomato purée and stock. Bring to the boil, reduce the heat, cover and simmer gently for 4 minutes.

Add the pasta and simmer for about 2 minutes more, until the pasta is al dente, tender with a bit of bite (not soft). Add salt and pepper to taste and serve.

Serves 4

cream of tomato soup

see variations page 163

Such a classic and so incredibly easy to make – you can whip up this delicious soup in no time. Serve it as as an elegant appetiser or a simple lunch with crusty bread.

2 tbsp olive oil
1 onion, chopped
3 garlic cloves, crushed
Two 400-g (14-oz) cans chopped tomatoes
570 ml (1 pt) vegetable stock

2 handfuls fresh basil, plus extra leaves to
  garnish
120 ml (4 fl oz) double cream
About $\frac{1}{4}$ tsp caster sugar
Salt and ground black pepper

Heat the oil in a large saucepan. Add the onion and garlic, and cook gently for 4 minutes. Stir in the tomatoes and stock, and bring to the boil. Then reduce the heat, cover and simmer for 10 minutes.

Pour the soup into a food processor or blender, add the basil and blend until smooth. Return the soup to the saucepan, stir in about two-thirds of the cream and warm through without boiling. Stir in sugar, salt and pepper to taste.

Ladle the soup into bowls and serve drizzled with the remaining cream and garnished with a few fresh basil leaves.

Serves 4

spring leaf soup

see variations page 164

Tender spring leaves take only minutes to cook and taste delicious blended into a refreshing, green soup.

1 large potato, diced
900 ml (1½ pts) vegetable stock
2 bunches spring onions, sliced
140 g (5 oz) spinach, roughly shredded
85 g (3 oz) rocket, roughly shredded
85 g (3 oz) sorrel, roughly shredded

200 ml (7 fl oz) white wine
120 ml (4 fl oz) double cream, plus extra for
    serving (optional)
Salt and ground black pepper
Finely shredded spinach or sorrel, to garnish

Put the potato and stock in a large saucepan. Bring to the boil, then reduce the heat, cover and simmer for about 5 minutes, until the potato is tender. Add the spring onions, spinach, rocket and sorrel. Cover and simmer for 2 to 3 minutes, until the leaves are wilted.

Pour the soup into a food processor or blender and process to a smooth purée. Return to the saucepan, stir in the wine and cream, and warm through. Add salt and pepper to taste and serve ladled into bowls. Drizzle with a little extra cream, if liked, and garnish with finely shredded spinach or sorrel.

Serves 4

asian-style prawn & noodle broth

see variations page 165

You can use any noodles you like for this soup — fine rice or wheat noodles work particularly well.

2 tbsp sunflower oil
3 shallots, finely chopped
2 tsp grated fresh root ginger
1 green chilli, seeded and finely chopped
2 tsp Thai green curry paste
1.2 l (2 pts) vegetable stock
175 g (6 oz) noodles

2 tsp soft brown sugar
Juice of about ½ lime, to taste
250 g (9 oz) peeled cooked tiger prawns
1 bunch spring onions, sliced at an angle
4 handfuls beansprouts
Large handful of fresh coriander leaves, plus
    extra to garnish

Heat the oil in a large saucepan. Add the shallots, ginger, chilli and curry paste, and cook gently for 2 minutes. Stir in the stock, bring to the boil, cover and simmer for 10 minutes. Meanwhile, cook the noodles in a separate saucepan of boiling water according to the packet instructions. Drain and set aside.

Stir the sugar and lime juice into the broth. Add the prawns and noodles and warm through. Add the beansprouts and spring onions, and stir in the coriander. Ladle the soup into bowls and serve immediately.

Serves 4

cream of chicken & saffron soup

see variations page 166

Incredibly quick and easy to make, yet luxurious and sophisticated, this soup makes a perfect speedy appetiser for an elegant dinner.

2 tbsp olive oil
1 onion, finely chopped
2 garlic cloves, crushed
300 g (10½ oz) skinless, boneless cooked
    chicken, cut into small bite-size pieces
800 ml (28 fl oz) chicken stock

200 ml (7 fl oz) white wine
Good pinch of saffron strands
200 ml (7 fl oz) double cream
Salt and ground black pepper
2 tbsp snipped fresh chives

Heat the oil in a large saucepan. Add the onion and garlic, and cook for 5 minutes. Add the chicken, stock and wine, and bring to the boil. Reduce the heat, cover the saucepan and simmer for 5 minutes. Stir in the saffron strands and cook for 1 minute.

Remove the saucepan from the heat and stir in the cream. Season to taste with salt and pepper, then ladle the soup into bowls. Serve sprinkled with chives.

Serves 4

celery soup with sherry

see variations page 167

Sherry brings an interesting edge to the flavour of this smooth, creamy soup, studded with chunks of tender, mild celery.

1 head of celery
40 g (1½ oz) butter
1 onion, finely chopped
2 tbsp plain flour
1 l (1¾ pts) chicken or vegetable stock

175 ml (6 fl oz) sherry
120 ml (4 fl oz) double cream
2 tbsp chopped fresh parsley
Salt and ground black pepper

Cut 1 celery stick into short fine sticks and set aside for garnishing the soup. Thinly slice the remaining celery and set aside.

Melt the butter in a large saucepan. Add the onion and cook gently for 4 minutes. Stir in the flour and cook for 1 minute, then gradually stir in the stock. Add the sliced celery and bring to the boil. Then reduce the heat, cover the saucepan and simmer for about 10 minutes, until the celery is tender.

Pour half the soup into a food processor or blender and process until smooth, then return it to the saucepan. Stir in the sherry, cream and parsley, and warm through without boiling. Add salt and pepper to taste and serve garnished with celery sticks.

Serves 4

variations

broccoli soup with parmesan toasts

see base recipe page 139

cauliflower soup with parmesan toasts
Prepare the basic recipe, using cauliflower in place of the broccoli.

broccoli & cauliflower soup with parmesan toasts
Prepare the basic recipe, using 225 g (8 oz) broccoli and
225 g (8 oz) cauliflower.

chunky broccoli soup with parmesan toasts
Prepare the basic recipe, removing about a quarter of the cooked broccoli
florets from the saucepan before processing the soup. Return the broccoli
florets to the saucepan with the milk and nutmeg.

broccoli & spinach soup with parmesan toasts
Prepare the basic recipe, using 350 g (12 oz) broccoli and 250 g
(9 oz) spinach. Add the spinach about 4 minutes after the broccoli.

courgette & broccoli soup with parmesan toasts
Prepare the basic recipe, using 250 g (9 oz) courgettes and
350 g (12 oz) broccoli.

variations

spiced chickpea & lemon soup

see base recipe page 141

spiced borlotti bean & lemon soup
Prepare the basic recipe, using borlotti beans in place of the chickpeas.

spiced flageolet bean & lemon soup
Prepare the basic recipe, using flageolet beans in place of the chickpeas.

spiced chickpea & lemon soup with fresh coriander
Prepare the basic recipe, using chopped fresh coriander in place of
the parsley.

spiced flageolet bean & lemon soup
Prepare the basic recipe, using flageolet beans in place of the chickpeas.

fiery chickpea & lemon soup
Prepare the basic recipe, stirring in ½ teaspoon crushed dried red chillies
with the spices.

variations

crab & sweetcorn chowder

see base recipe page 142

crab & sweetcorn chowder with spring onions
Prepare the basic recipe, stirring in 4 sliced spring onions in place of
the parsley.

crab, sweetcorn & green pepper chowder
Prepare the basic recipe, adding 1 seeded, finely chopped green pepper in
place of the red pepper.

tuna & sweetcorn chowder
Prepare the basic recipe, adding two 170-g (6-oz) cans tuna fish, drained, in
place of the crabmeat.

mussel & sweetcorn chowder
Prepare the basic recipe, using 350 g (12 oz) cooked, shelled mussels in place
of the crabmeat.

prawn & sweetcorn chowder
Prepare the basic recipe, using 350 g (12 oz) peeled cooked prawns in place
of the crabmeat.

variations

cappelletti in brodo

see base recipe page 145

cappelletti in brodo with chicken
Prepare the basic recipe, adding 1 shredded, cooked skinless chicken breast
to the broth.

cappelletti in brodo with roast peppers
Prepare the basic recipe, adding 3 sliced, bottled, roast peppers to the broth.

fagotini in brodo
Prepare the basic recipe, using mushroom fagotini in place of the cappelleti,
and vegetable stock in place of the chicken stock.

cappelletti in brodo with beans
Prepare the basic recipe, adding a 400-g (14-oz) can rinsed, drained borlotti
beans to the broth.

variations

fresh vegetable minestrone

see base recipe page 146

fresh vegetable minestrone with pesto
Prepare the basic recipe and serve topped with a spoonful of pesto.

fresh vegetable minestrone with green beans
Prepare the basic recipe, adding 100 g (3½ oz) green beans, cut into
3 cm (1¼ in) lengths, in place of the courgette.

fresh vegetable minestrone with flageolet beans
Prepare the basic recipe, adding a 400-g (14-oz) can drained, rinsed
flageolet beans with the vegetables.

fresh vegetable minestrone with bacon
Prepare the basic recipe, frying 3 roughly chopped rindless bacon rashers
with the onion and garlic.

fresh vegetable minestrone with chicken
Prepare the basic recipe, adding 1 shredded skinless cooked chicken breast
with the vegetables, and using chicken stock in place of the vegetable stock.

variations

cream of tomato soup

see base recipe page 149

cream of tomato & pepper soup
Prepare the basic recipe, adding 2 seeded chopped red peppers
with the tomatoes.

red-hot cream of tomato soup
Prepare the basic recipe, frying 2 seeded, chopped red chillies with the onion
and garlic.

cream of tomato soup with fresh coriander
Prepare the basic recipe, using fresh coriander in place of the basil.

cream of tomato soup with fresh mint
Prepare the basic recipe, using 1 tablespoon chopped fresh mint in place of
the basil, and garnishing with fresh mint leaves.

fresh tomato soup
Prepare the basic recipe, using 800 g (1 lb 5 oz) peeled, chopped fresh
tomatoes in place of canned tomatoes.

variations

spring leaf soup

see base recipe page 150

spinach & rocket soup
Prepare the basic recipe, using 140 g (5 oz) each of spinach and rocket, and omitting the sorrel.

spring leaf soup with artichoke bruschetta
Prepare the basic recipe. Serve with artichoke bruschetta: toast 8 slices of baguette until golden on both sides, then spread each with a little pesto and top with a bottled, chargrilled artichoke heart.

spring leaf soup with red onion
Prepare the basic recipe, using 1 finely chopped red onion in place of the spring onions. Serve garnished with more chopped red onion.

spring leaf & watercress soup
Prepare the basic recipe, adding a large handful of shredded watercress with the other leaves.

variations

asian-style prawn & noodle broth

see base recipe page 153

asian-style chicken & noodle broth
Prepare the basic recipe, using chicken stock in place of the vegetable stock, and adding 2 shredded, skinless cooked chicken breasts in place of the prawns.

asian-style prawn & noodle broth with coconut milk
Prepare the basic recipe using 800 ml (28 fl oz) stock and 400 ml (14 fl oz) coconut milk.

asian-style prawn & noodle broth with fresh basil
Prepare the basic recipe, using fresh basil in place of the coriander.

asian-style prawn & noodle broth with fresh mint
Prepare the basic recipe, using 1 tablespoon chopped fresh mint in place of the coriander, and fresh mint leaves to garnish.

variations

cream of chicken & saffron soup

see base recipe page 154

cream of chicken & saffron soup with tomatoes
Prepare the basic recipe, adding 3 peeled, seeded and chopped tomatoes with the stock.

cream of chicken & saffron soup with parsley
Prepare the basic soup, using parsley in place of the chives.

cream of chicken & saffron soup with spring onions
Prepare the basic soup, stirring in 1 bunch sliced spring onions with the saffron threads.

spiced cream of chicken & saffron soup
Prepare the basic soup, frying 1 chopped, seeded red chilli with the onions and garlic.

variations

celery soup with sherry

see base recipe page 157

celery soup with white wine
Prepare the basic recipe, using white wine in place of the sherry.

celery & chicken soup with sherry
Prepare the basic recipe, adding 300 g (10½ oz) skinless cooked chicken, cut into bite-size pieces, with the celery.

celery & pheasant soup with sherry
Prepare the basic recipe, adding 300 g (10½ oz) cooked pheasant meat, cut into bite-size pieces, with the celery.

celery & tomato soup with sherry
Prepare the basic soup, adding 3 peeled, seeded and chopped tomatoes with the celery.

fennel soup with sherry
Prepare the basic recipe, using 2 sliced fennel bulbs in place of the celery.

hot & spicy

Hot chillies and warm spices were just made to go in soups. From all over the world, every country has its own traditions – take your pick from the hot and peppery or warm and spicy flavours packed into the soups into this chapter.

moroccan harira

see variations page 188

There are countless variations of this soup, which is served in the evening during the 30-day fast of Ramadan. This recipe, with lentils and chicken, is spiced, but not too hot.

100 g (3½ oz) Puy lentils
2 tbsp olive oil
1 onion, finely chopped
2 garlic cloves, crushed
½ tsp ground ginger
2 tsp ground cinnamon
½ tsp ground turmeric
1 tsp harissa
1.2 l (2 pts) chicken stock

400-g (14-oz) can chopped tomatoes
1 tbsp tomato purée
400-g (14-oz) can chickpeas, drained
2 skinless, boneless chicken breasts, cut into
    bite-size strips
Juice of ¼ to ½ lemon
Salt and ground black pepper
Handful of fresh coriander, chopped, to serve

Cook the lentils in plenty of boiling water for 25 minutes. Drain and set aside. Heat the oil in a large saucepan. Add the onions and garlic, and cook gently for 5 minutes. Stir in the ginger, cinnamon, turmeric and harissa, then pour in the stock. Add the tomatoes, tomato purée, chickpeas and lentils.

Bring the soup to the boil, reduce the heat and cover. Cook for about 15 minutes. Add the chicken and cook for a further 5 to 10 minutes, until the chicken is cooked through. Squeeze in lemon juice and salt and pepper to taste. Serve scattered with chopped fresh coriander.

Serves 4

curried parsnip soup

see variations page 189

This hearty, warming winter soup is a real classic. Sweet, fragrant parsnips go wonderfully with Indian-style spicing. You can serve with any bread, but wedges of naan complement the Indian flavour.

2 tbsp sunflower oil
3 garlic cloves, crushed
1 onion, chopped
2 green chillies, seeded and chopped
1 tsp ground cumin
1 tsp ground coriander
½ tsp ground ginger

½ tsp ground turmeric
5 parsnips, peeled and chopped
1.2 l (2 pts) vegetable or chicken stock
Juice of about ½ lemon, to taste
Salt and ground black pepper
Plain yoghurt and wedges of naan bread, to serve
1 tbsp chopped fresh mint, to sprinkle

Heat the oil in a large saucepan. Add the garlic, onion and chilli, and cook gently for 4 minutes. Stir in the cumin, coriander, ginger, turmeric and parsnips, then pour in the stock. Bring to the boil and reduce the heat. Simmer the soup for about 20 minutes, until the parsnips are tender.

Process the soup in a food processor or blender until smooth. Stir in lemon juice and salt and pepper to taste. Serve the soup topped with a little yoghurt and sprinkled with mint, with wedges of naan bread on the side.

Serves 4

indian-inspired mulligatawny

see variations page 190

Created in India at the time of the British Raj, this creamy lentil soup, enriched with coconut milk, takes its name from Tamil word for 'pepper water'.

2 tbsp sunflower oil
1 onion, finely chopped
3 garlic cloves, crushed
2 hot green chillies, seeded and chopped
2 tsp ground cumin
1 tsp ground coriander
1 tsp turmeric
½ tsp ground cinnamon
1 l (1¾ pts) vegetable stock

400 ml (14 fl oz) coconut milk
115 g (4 oz) red lentils
2 celery sticks, chopped
2 carrots, chopped
1 apple, chopped
Juice of about ¼ lemon, to taste
Salt and ground black pepper
Handful of fresh coriander leaves

Heat the oil in a large saucepan. Add the onion and garlic, and cook for about 4 minutes. Stir in the chillies, cumin, coriander, turmeric and cinnamon, followed by the stock, coconut milk, lentils, celery, carrots and apple. Bring to the boil, then reduce the heat, cover and simmer for about 30 minutes, until the lentils are tender.

Stir in lemon juice and salt and pepper to taste. Ladle the soup into serving bowls and sprinkle with fresh coriander.

Serves 4

spiced carrot soup

see variations page 191

Inspired by the flavours of Morocco, this spiced carrot soup is delicious with wedges of toasted pitta bread, or Middle-Eastern flatbread as a meal, or on its own as an appetiser.

2 tbsp sunflower oil
1 onion, chopped
3 garlic cloves, crushed
2 tsp ground cumin
1 tsp ground coriander
½ tsp ground ginger
1 tsp paprika
Good pinch of cayenne pepper

1 small potato, diced
500 g (1 lb 2 oz) carrots, sliced
1.2 l (2 pts) vegetable or chicken stock
Juice of 1 orange
1 to 1½ tbsp red wine vinegar
Salt and ground black pepper
Handful of fresh coriander, chopped

Heat the oil in a large saucepan. Add the onion and garlic, and cook gently for 4 minutes. Stir in the cumin, coriander, ginger, paprika and cayenne pepper, then add the potato, carrots and stock.

Bring to the boil, reduce the heat and cover the saucepan. Simmer for about 20 minutes, until the vegetables are tender. Process the soup in a food processor or blender until smooth. Stir in the orange juice, then add vinegar, salt and pepper to taste. Ladle the soup into bowls, sprinkle with coriander and serve.

Serves 4

roast squash soup with coconut milk & thai spices

see variations page 192

Sweet, tender roast squash, fragrant Thai spices and creamy coconut milk make a delicious combination in this chunky soup.

1 butternut squash, seeded, peeled and cut into chunks
3 tbsp sunflower oil
2 shallots, finely chopped
2 garlic cloves, crushed
2 tsp grated fresh root ginger
2 green chillies, seeded and shredded, plus extra to garnish

2 lemongrass stalks, chopped
4 kaffir lime leaves, shredded
800 ml (28 fl oz) vegetable stock
400 ml (14 fl oz) coconut milk
Juice of about 1 lime
1 tbsp fish sauce
Handful of fresh coriander leaves

Preheat the oven to 200°C (400°F / Gas 6). Put the squash in a baking dish, drizzle with 1 tablespoon of the oil and toss to coat. Roast for about 25 minutes, until tender.

Heat the remaining oil in a large saucepan. Add the shallots, garlic and ginger, and cook gently for about 3 minutes. Add the chillies, lemongrass, lime leaves, stock and coconut milk, and bring to the boil. Reduce the heat, cover and simmer for about 20 minutes. Add the squash to the soup, then stir in lime juice and fish sauce to taste. Serve ladled into bowls, sprinkled with fresh coriander.

Serves 4

hot chilli-squid soup

see variations page 193

Chillies, tomatoes and squid seem to be a partnership made in heaven, and they are divine in this light tomato broth.

6 squid, cleaned
Juice of 1 lemon
3 tbsp olive oil
3 shallots, finely chopped
2 hot red chillies, seeded and chopped
450 g (1 lb) ripe tomatoes, peeled, seeded and chopped

1.2 l (2 pts) fish or vegetable stock
1 tbsp tomato purée
½ tsp ground cinnamon
Pinch of soft light brown sugar
1 tbsp chopped fresh mint
Salt and ground black pepper

Separate the tentacles from the squid in one piece. Discard the head. Slice the bodies into rings and put in a bowl with the tentacles and lemon juice. Cover and chill for 30 minutes.

Heat 2 tbsp of the oil in a large saucepan. Add the shallots and chillies, and cook gently for 2 minutes. Add the tomatoes, stock, tomato purée and cinnamon. Bring to the boil, reduce the heat, cover and simmer for 10 minutes. Process the soup in blender or food processor until smooth, then return it to the pan. Add sugar and salt and pepper to taste; keep warm.

Drain the squid, pat dry on paper towels, then season with salt and pepper. Heat the remaining oil in a non-stick frying pan. Fry the squid for 1 minute, until just cooked. Ladle the soup into bowls, spoon the squid on top, sprinkle with fresh mint and serve.

Serves 4

spicy chicken gumbo soup

see variations page 194

This classic cross between stew and soup is traditionally served ladled over cooked rice to make a substantial meal. Serve it without rice for a lighter lunch or supper.

2 tbsp olive oil
1 onion, chopped
2 garlic cloves, finely chopped
1½ tbsp plain flour
1.2 l (2 pts) chicken stock
2 green peppers, seeded and chopped
200 g (7 oz) okra, trimmed and cut
    into 5 to 10 mm (¼ to ½ in) slices
4 ripe tomatoes, peeled and chopped

2 tbsp tomato purée
1 tsp fresh thyme
1 tsp cayenne pepper
300 g (10½ oz) cooked skinless chicken,
    cut into bite-size pieces
115 g (4 oz) sweetcorn
Salt and ground black pepper
Tabasco sauce, to taste
Boiled rice, to serve

Heat the oil in a large saucepan. Add the onion and garlic, and cook gently for about 4 minutes. Stir in the flour and cook for a further 1 minute. Gradually stir in the chicken stock, followed by the peppers, okra, tomatoes, tomato purée, thyme and cayenne pepper. Bring the soup to the boil, then reduce the heat, cover and simmer for about 30 minutes, stirring occasionally.

Stir in the chicken and corn, and cook for a further 30 minutes, stirring occasionally. Add salt and pepper, and tabasco sauce to taste. Serve the soup ladled over rice.

Serves 4

spicy cauliflower & potato soup

see variations page 195

Coconut and Indian-style spice mixtures taste terrific with the cauliflower and potatoes in this chunky soup.

2 tbsp sunflower oil
1 onion, finely chopped
2 green chillies, seeded and chopped
2 garlic cloves, finely chopped
2 tsp grated fresh root ginger
2 tsp ground cumin
1 tsp ground coriander
½ tsp ground turmeric
800 ml (28 fl oz) vegetable or chicken stock

400 ml (14 fl oz) coconut milk
300 g (10½ oz) potatoes, peeled and cut into cubes
300 g (10½ oz) cauliflower, broken into bite-size florets
Salt and ground black pepper
Juice of about ½ lemon, to taste
Handful of fresh coriander, chopped

Heat the oil in a saucepan. Add and cook the onion, chillies, garlic and ginger for 4 minutes. Stir in the cumin, coriander and turmeric. Add the stock, coconut milk, potatoes and cauliflower. Bring to the boil, reduce the heat, cover and simmer gently for 10 to 15 minutes.

When the vegetables are tender, ladle half of them into a blender or food processor and process until smooth, then stir this purée back into the soup. Add salt, pepper and lemon juice to taste. Ladle the soup into bowls, sprinkle with fresh coriander and serve.

Serves 4

red-hot spicy chickpea & pasta soup

see variations page 196

This chunky, wholesome soup has a real bite – making it perfect for serving on a cold day when you really need to warm yourself up.

2 tbsp olive oil
3 red chillies, seeded and chopped
3 garlic cloves, crushed
6 ripe tomatoes, peeled and chopped
1 l (1¼ pts) vegetable or chicken stock
400-g (14-oz) can chickpeas, drained and rinsed

115 g (4 oz) soup pasta
Bunch of spring onions, sliced
1 tbsp chopped fresh mint
Salt
Parmesan cheese shavings, to serve

Heat the oil in a large saucepan. Add the chillies and garlic, and cook gently for 2 minutes. Stir in the tomatoes, stock and chickpeas, and bring to the boil. Reduce the heat, cover and simmer for about 20 minutes.

Add the pasta to the soup and simmer for a further 5 minutes, until tender. Stir in the spring onions, mint and salt to taste. Ladle the soup into bowls and serve immediately, sprinkled with Parmesan shavings.

Serves 4

ginger & tiger prawn soup

see variations page 197

Tender juicy prawns cooked in a fragrant broth and served with rice noodles taste divine and couldn't be easier to prepare.

2 tbsp sunflower oil
2 tsp grated fresh root ginger
2 garlic cloves, crushed
2 shallots, finely chopped
1.2 l (2 pts) fish or vegetable stock
2 tbsp sweet chilli sauce
115 g (4 oz) rice noodles

Juice of ½ to 1 lime, to taste
1 tsp Thai fish sauce
300 g (10½ oz) tiger prawns, peeled and deveined
Bunch of spring onions, sliced
Handful of fresh basil leaves, torn

Heat the oil in a large saucepan. Add the ginger, garlic and shallots, and cook for 2 minutes. Pour in the stock and chilli sauce, and bring to the boil. Reduce the heat, cover and simmer for about 20 minutes.

Towards the end of the cooking time, put the noodles in a medium bowl, pour boiling water over them and leave to soak for 5 minutes, until tender (following the packet instructions). Drain and set aside.

Stir in lime juice and fish sauce to taste. Add the prawns and cook for about 2 minutes, until the prawns are pink and cooked through. Stir in the spring onions and noodles. Ladle the soup into bowls, then scatter with the basil and serve immediately.

Serves 4

variations

moroccan harira

see base recipe page 169

vegetarian harira
Prepare the basic recipe, using vegetable stock in place of the chicken stock and omitting the chicken.

lamb harira
Prepare the basic recipe, using lamb or beef stock in place of the chicken stock, and cooked lamb in place of the chicken.

mixed vegetable harira
Prepare the basic recipe, adding 1 quartered, sliced courgette, 1 quartered sliced carrot and 1 finely diced red pepper with the chickpeas and chicken.

fiery harira
Prepare the basic recipe, adding ¼ to ½ teaspoon crushed dried red chilli with the spices.

variations

curried parsnip soup

see base recipe page 171

curried carrot soup
Prepare the basic recipe, using 5 large carrots and 1 small potato in place
of the parsnips.

simple curried parsnip soup
Prepare the basic recipe, using 1½ tablespoons curry paste in place of the
cumin, coriander, ginger and turmeric.

curried beetroot soup
Prepare the basic recipe, using 5 large peeled, chopped raw beetroot in place
of the parsnips.

curried parsnip & carrot soup
Prepare the basic recipe, using 3 parsnips and 3 large carrots.

variations

indian-inspired mulligatawny

see base recipe page 172

indian-inspired mulligatawny with chicken
Prepare the basic recipe, using chicken stock in place of the vegetable stock. Add 300 g (10½ oz) shredded skinless cooked chicken towards the end of cooking

indian-inspired mulligatawny with lamb
Prepare the basic recipe, using lamb stock in place of the vegetable stock. Add 300 g (10½ oz) shredded cooked lamb towards the end of cooking.

indian-inspired mulligatawny with tomatoes
Prepare the basic recipe, adding 4 ripe, peeled, chopped tomatoes with the other vegetables.

indian-inspired low-fat mulligatawny
Prepare the basic recipe, using 1.2 l (2 pts) vegetable stock and omitting the coconut milk. Serve topped with a swirl of low-fat plain yoghurt.

indian-inspired mulligatawny with fresh mint
Prepare the basic recipe, sprinkling the finished soup with a little chopped fresh mint in place of the coriander.

variations

spiced carrot soup

see base recipe page 175

chilled spiced carrot soup
Prepare the basic recipe, then leave to cool and chill for at least 4 hours before serving.

spiced carrot soup with harissa
Prepare the basic recipe, adding 1 teaspoon harissa in place of the paprika and cayenne pepper.

spiced carrot soup with mint
Prepare the basic recipe, sprinkling the soup with chopped fresh mint instead of coriander.

spiced carrot soup with soured cream
Prepare the basic recipe and serve each portion topped with a spoonful of soured cream.

spiced carrot & red pepper soup
Prepare the basic recipe, using 450 g (1 lb) carrots and 2 seeded, diced red peppers.

variations

roast squash soup with coconut milk & thai spices

see base recipe page 176

roast squash soup with coconut milk, thai spices & toasted cashew nuts
Prepare the basic recipe, scattering toasted cashew nuts over the soup
to serve.

velvet-smooth roast squash soup with coconut milk & thai spices
Prepare the basic recipe and process until smooth in a blender or food
processor before serving.

roast squash & prawn soup with coconut milk & thai spices
Prepare the basic recipe, adding 20 peeled cooked tiger prawns to the soup
with the squash.

roast squash & chicken soup with coconut milk & thai spices
Prepare the basic recipe, adding 300 g (10½ oz) cooked chicken, cut into bite-
size pieces, with the squash.

roast squash soup with noodles, coconut milk & thai spices
Prepare the basic recipe, and serve ladled over freshly cooked noodles.

variations

hot chilli-squid soup

see base recipe page 179

chunky hot chilli-squid soup
Prepare the basic recipe, but do not blend the soup — serve it chunky,
topped with the squid and mint.

hot chilli-squid soup with coriander
Prepare the basic recipe, sprinkling the soup with chopped fresh coriander
in place of the mint.

garlic chilli-squid soup
Prepare the basic recipe, using 3 crushed garlic cloves in place of the
shallots. Fry the garlic with the chilli for about 1 minute, then add the
tomatoes and stock and continue as in the main recipe.

tomato & ginger soup with squid
Prepare the basic recipe, using 2 teaspoons grated fresh root ginger
in place of the chillies.

variations

spicy chicken gumbo soup

see base recipe page 180

vegetarian spicy gumbo soup
Prepare the basic recipe, using vegetable stock in place of the chicken stock, and omitting the chicken.

spicy chicken gumbo soup with green beans
Prepare the basic recipe. About 10 minutes before the end of the cooking time, stir in 150 g (5 oz) trimmed green beans cut into 2 cm (¾ in) lengths.

green chilli chicken gumbo soup
Prepare the basic recipe, frying 2 seeded, chopped green chillies with the onion and garlic. Use half the amount of cayenne pepper.

spicy chicken gumbo with fresh mint
Prepare the basic recipe, sprinkling the soup with chopped fresh mint before serving.

variations

spicy cauliflower & potato soup

see base recipe page 183

smooth spicy cauliflower & potato soup
Prepare the basic recipe and process the whole batch of soup until smooth before serving.

spicy cauliflower, potato & chickpea soup
Prepare the basic recipe, using half the quantity of potato and adding a 400-g (14-oz) can drained, rinsed chickpeas with the potato and cauliflower.

spicy cauliflower & potato soup with naan
Prepare the basic recipe and serve the soup with wedges of naan bread.

spicy cauliflower & potato soup with yoghurt & mango chutney
Prepare the basic recipe and serve bowls of soup topped with a spoonful of plain yoghurt and a dollop of mango chutney.

spicy cauliflower & carrot soup
Prepare the basic recipe, using carrots in place of the potatoes.

variations

red-hot spicy chickpea & pasta soup

see base recipe page 184

red-hot kidney bean & pasta soup
Prepare the basic recipe, using kidney beans in place of the chickpeas.

Red-hot chickpea & vermicelli soup
Prepare the basic recipe, using vermicelli in place of the soup pasta.

Red-hot flageolet bean & pasta soup
Prepare the basic recipe, using flageolet beans in place of the chickpeas.

Green hot chickpea & pasta soup
Prepare the basic recipe, using green chillies in place of red.

Red-hot chickpea & pasta soup with bacon
Prepare the basic recipe, frying 2 roughly chopped rindless bacon rashers with the chilli and garlic.

variations

ginger & tiger prawn soup

see base recipe page 187

ginger & salmon soup
Prepare the basic recipe, omitting the prawns. Grill 4 portions of salmon fillet while the soup cooks. Place the noodles in bowls, top with the salmon and ladle over the broth.

spicy ginger & tiger prawn soup
Prepare the basic recipe, frying 1 seeded, chopped red chilli with the ginger, garlic and shallots.

fragrant ginger & tiger prawn soup
Prepare the basic recipe, adding 2 chopped lemongrass stalks with the stock, and scattering the finished soup with a handful of coriander leaves in place of the basil.

ginger & tiger prawn soup with chives
Prepare the basic recipe, scattering ½ tablespoon snipped fresh chives over each bowl of soup in place of the basil.

ginger & tiger prawn soup with fresh mint
Prepare the basic recipe, scattering 1 teaspoon chopped fresh mint over each bowl of soup in place of the basil.

sophisticated starters

When you're entertaining or just want to make

a special meal, a bowl of prettily garnished soup

to start is just what you need. Try any one of these

stunning soups in this chapter and you're sure

to feel like the host with the most.

spiced cherry tomato & vodka soup with seared scallops

see variations page 216

Sweet, tender seared scallops, marinated in ginger and lime, are a real gourmet treat – perfect for dressing up a simple tomato soup.

2 tbsp sunflower oil, plus extra for frying
2 shallots, finely chopped
2 garlic cloves, crushed
2 hot fresh red chillies, finely chopped
500 g (1 lb 2 oz) cherry tomatoes
1 l (1¾ pts) vegetable stock

1 tsp grated fresh root ginger
Juice of 1 lime
1 tsp chopped fresh mint, plus extra to garnish
Salt
12 scallops, shelled and cleaned
2 tbsp vodka

Heat the oil in a large saucepan. Add the shallots, garlic and chillies. Cook for 2 minutes. Add the tomatoes and stock. Bring to the boil, reduce the heat, cover and simmer for 10 minutes.

Combine the ginger, lime juice, mint and a pinch of salt and pour the liquid over the scallops. Set aside until the soup is cooked. Process the soup in a blender until smooth, then strain it back into the rinsed-out pan. Add salt and keep warm.

Heat a non-stick frying pan. Add a drizzle of oil. Add the scallops and marinade, and sear on each side for 1 minute, until just cooked. Stir the vodka into the soup and ladle it into bowls. Pile three scallops in the centre of each portion. Sprinkle with a little mint and serve.

Serves 4

garden pea soup with prosciutto croûtes

see variations page 217

Frozen peas that are frozen almost as soon as they are picked often have a better flavour than fresh vegetables, and they are perfect in this luxurious, yet simple, soup.

2 tbsp olive oil
2 shallots, chopped
1 garlic clove, crushed
600 g (1 lb 5 oz) frozen peas
700 ml (24 fl oz) vegetable or chicken stock
4 tbsp double cream
Salt and ground black pepper

for the croûtes

2 tbsp good-quality mayonnaise
¼ tsp Dijon mustard
¼ tsp grated lemon rind
4 small slices baguette
2 strips prosciutto, halved

Heat the oil in a large saucepan. Add the shallots and garlic, and cook gently for about 2 minutes. Add the peas and stock, and bring to the boil. Remove from the heat and process the soup in a food processor or blender until smooth. Stir in the cream and season to taste.

Meanwhile, prepare the croûtes. Combine the mayonnaise, mustard and lemon rind. Toast the bread slices on both sides until golden, then leave to cool.

To serve, ladle the soup into bowls. Top each toast with a dollop of mayonnaise and curl a strip of prosciutto on top. Grind over a little black pepper and serve with the soup.

Serves 4

spicy crab & coconut soup

see variations page 218

Choose red-hot bird's eye chillies to add a real bite to this rich, creamy soup with its delicious chunks of crabmeat. Small bowlfuls are ample for an appetiser.

2 tbsp sunflower oil
3 shallots, finely chopped
2 tsp grated fresh root ginger
2 lemongrass stalks, chopped
2 green chillies, seeded and finely chopped
1 l (1¾ pts) vegetable stock

120 ml (4 fl oz) coconut cream
4 spring onions, sliced
Two 170-g (6-oz) cans crabmeat
Juice of ¼ to ½ lime, to taste
Salt and ground black pepper
Handful of fresh coriander leaves, chopped

Heat the oil in a large saucepan. Add the shallots, ginger, lemongrass and chillies, and cook gently for about 2 minutes. Pour in the stock and bring to the boil. Reduce the heat, cover and simmer the soup gently for about 20 minutes.

Stir in the coconut cream, then add the spring onions and crabmeat. Warm the soup, without allowing it to boil, for about 2 minutes. Add lime juice, salt and pepper to taste. Ladle the soup into bowls and sprinkle with fresh coriander.

Serves 4

broad bean & mange tout soup

see variations page 219

Light and fresh, this is a lovely soup to make in summer, when broad beans and mange tout are in abundance and at their best.

2 tbsp olive oil
2 shallots, finely chopped
2 garlic cloves, crushed
6 ripe tomatoes, peeled and chopped
1.15 litres (2 pts) vegetable stock

450 g (1 lb) fresh, broad beans, shelled
200 g (7 oz) mange tout, sliced
Handful of fresh basil leaves, torn
Salt and ground black pepper

Heat the oil in a large saucepan. Add the shallots and garlic, and cook gently, stirring occasionally, for 2 to 3 minutes. Add the tomatoes and stock and bring to the boil. Reduce the heat, cover and simmer gently for 10 minutes.

Add the beans and mange tout to the soup. Simmer for about 3 minutes, until the vegetables are just tender, but still have a crisp bite. Add the basil and salt and pepper to taste, then serve the soup ladled into bowls.

Serves 4

creamed artichoke soup with anchovy toasts

see variations page 220

There's something rather special about artichokes, and this simple soup, made using canned artichoke hearts, takes all the hassle out of the preparation.

2 tbsp olive oil, plus extra for
    drizzling
1 onion, chopped
3 garlic cloves, chopped
2 tsp ground cumin
Two 400-g (14-oz) cans artichoke
    hearts, drained
1.15 l (2 pts) vegetable stock

2 tsp chopped fresh mint, plus extra to garnish
Salt and ground black pepper

for the anchovy toasts

4 anchovy fillets
55 g (2 oz) butter, at room temperature
8 slices baguette

Heat the oil in a large saucepan. Add the onion and garlic, and cook gently for 4 minutes. Stir in the cumin, then add the artichoke hearts and stock. Bring to the boil, reduce the heat and cover the saucepan. Simmer the soup for 10 minutes, then process it in a food processor or blender until smooth. Stir in the mint and check the seasoning.

Crush the anchovy fillets with a spoon, then beat in the butter. Toast the bread on both sides. Spread with anchovy butter and season with black pepper. Ladle the soup into bowls, sprinkle with mint and float a toast in each portion; offer the remaining toasts on the side.

Serves 4

vermouth & fennel soup

see variations page 221

Vermouth, with its herb-like aroma, is a perfect partner for delicate fennel in this light, yet creamy, soup. Serve with wafer-thin slices of toasted sourdough bread.

2 tbsp olive oil, plus extra for brushing
1 onion, chopped
450 g (1 lb) fennel bulbs
750 ml (1¼ pts) vegetable stock
120 ml (4 fl oz) vermouth

4 tbsp double cream
Salt and ground black pepper

Heat the oil in a large saucepan. Add the onion and cook gently for about 4 minutes. Trim any fronds from the fennel and reserve them for garnish, and then chop the bulbs. Add the fennel and stock to the saucepan and bring to the boil. Reduce the heat, cover and simmer for about 15 minutes, until the fennel is tender.

Process the soup in a food processor or blender until smooth. Return it to the saucepan and pour in the vermouth. Stir in the cream, add salt and pepper to taste and warm the soup through without boiling.

Ladle the soup into bowls and sprinkle with the reserved fennel fronds, then serve immediately, while piping hot.

Serves 4

asparagus soup with smoked salmon crostini

see variations page 222

Light, creamy and delicate with the distinctive taste of asparagus, this simple soup has elegant crostini floating on top to make a stunning first course for any special meal.

600 g (1 lb 5 oz) asparagus
40 g (1½ oz) butter
1 onion, finely chopped
1½ tbsp plain flour
1 l (1¾ pts) vegetable stock
5 tbsp double cream

Juice of about ¼ lemon, to taste
4 slices small baguette, toasted until golden
2 tbsp mayonnaise
1 slice smoked salmon, cut into 4 strips
Salt and ground black pepper

Cut off and reserve the asparagus tips, then slice the stems. Melt the butter in a large saucepan. Add the onion and cook for 4 minutes. Stir in the flour and cook for 1 minute, then gradually stir in the stock. Add the asparagus stems and bring to the boil. Reduce the heat, cover and simmer for about 10 minutes, until the asparagus is tender.

Meanwhile, cook the asparagus tips in boiling water for 2 to 6 minutes, until tender. Drain and refresh under cold water. Process the soup in a food processor or blender until smooth, then return it to the pan. Stir in the cream, lemon juice and salt and pepper to taste, and all but four of the asparagus tips. Heat without boiling. Ladle the soup into bowls. Top the toasts with mayonnaise, smoked salmon and asparagus tips. Float the crostini in the soups..

Serves 4

rich porcini soup with sherry & nutmeg

see variations page 223

Porcini mushrooms have a wonderfully rich, smoky flavour. This soup uses dried mushrooms, so you can enjoy it all year round, not only when porcini are in season.

25 g (1 oz) dried porcini
240 ml (8 fl oz) boiling water
40 g (1½ oz) butter
1 onion, chopped
3 garlic cloves, crushed
1 tbsp plain flour
1.2 l (2 pts) vegetable stock

450 g (1 lb) chestnut mushrooms, sliced
120 ml (4 fl oz) sherry
120 ml (4 fl oz) double cream
1 tsp freshly grated nutmeg
Salt and ground black pepper
Chopped fresh parsley, to garnish

Soak the porcini in the boiling water for 20 minutes. Melt the butter in a saucepan. Add the onion and garlic, and cook gently for 4 minutes. Stir in the flour and cook for 1 minute, then gradually stir in the stock. Add the chestnut mushrooms, porcini and their soaking water. Bring to the boil, reduce the heat, cover and simmer for 20 minutes.

Remove a ladleful of the mushrooms from the saucepan, then pour the rest of the soup into a food processor or blender. Process until smooth, then return the soup to the saucepan and stir in the sherry, cream, nutmeg and reserved mushrooms. Add salt and pepper to taste and warm through without boiling. Serve garnished with parsley.

Serves 4

sweet pepper & salmon soup with fresh basil

see variations page 224

Fresh and tangy with the taste of peppers and orange, this stunning bright orange-red soup, flecked with green basil, makes a fabulous appetiser for a special dinner.

2 tbsp olive oil
1 onion, chopped
2 garlic cloves, crushed
3 red peppers, seeded and chopped
3 yellow peppers, seeded and chopped
2 tsp ground coriander

1.2 l (2 pts) vegetable stock
Juice of 2 oranges
2 salmon fillets, skinned
Handful of fresh basil leaves, torn, plus extra, to garnish
Salt and ground black pepper

Heat the olive oil in a large saucepan. Add the onion and garlic and cook for 4 minutes. Add the peppers and fry gently for 5 minutes. Stir in the coriander, then add the stock and orange juice, and bring to the boil. Reduce the heat, cover and simmer for about 20 minutes.

Meanwhile, poach the salmon in a shallow saucepan of barely simmering water for about 8 minutes, until just cooked. Use a fish slice to transfer the fish to a plate and leave until cool enough to handle. Flake the fish into large pieces and set aside.

Process the soup in a food processor or blender until smooth. Add the basil and salmon, with salt and pepper to taste. Ladle the soup into bowls and serve sprinkled with fresh basil.

Serves 4

classic beef consommé

see variations page 225

This old-fashioned appetiser still makes a truly sophisticated opening to a meal. The crystal-clear broth has a wonderfully rich flavour – perfect for whetting the appetite.

1.7 l (3 pints) beef stock
2 shallots, chopped
2 leeks, sliced
2 celery sticks, sliced
2 carrots, chopped
300 g (10½ oz) lean minced beef

2 egg whites
2 egg shells, crushed
2 tbsp sherry
Salt and ground black pepper
Finely shredded celery, to garnish (optional)

Bring the stock to the boil in a large saucepan. In a separate large saucepan, mix the shallots, leeks, celery, carrots, beef, egg whites and egg shells. Whisk in the stock, then bring to the boil, whisking all the time. Reduce the heat and simmer gently for 1 hour.

Scoop off the thick layer of scum from the surface of the broth. Scald a metal sieve, piece of muslin and clean saucepan or large bowl with boiling water. Line the sieve with the muslin and place it over the saucepan or bowl. Strain the stock through this sieve.

Stir in the sherry with salt and pepper to taste, then heat through and serve. Garnish with fine shreds of celery, if liked.

Serves 4

variations

spiced cherry tomato & vodka soup with seared scallops

see base recipe page 199

spiced cherry tomato & vodka soup with garlic scallops
Prepare the basic recipe, adding 1 crushed garlic clove to the marinade for the scallops.

spiced cherry tomato & vodka soup with seared squid
Prepare the basic recipe, using 6 cleaned squid in place of the scallops. Pull the tentacles from the body, then slice the body into rings and continue as before, searing for about 1 minute until just cooked.

spiced cherry tomato & vodka soup
Prepare the basic recipe, omitting the scallops.

spiced cherry tomato & vodka soup with prawns
Prepare the basic recipe, using 12 shelled, deveined raw tiger prawns in place of the scallops.

iced cherry tomato & vodka soup
Prepare the basic recipe, omitting the scallops. Leave the soup to cool, then chill it for at least 2 hours before serving.

garden pea soup with prosciutto croûtes

see base recipe page 201

garden pea soup with asparagus croutes
Prepare the basic recipe, using 4 cooked asparagus spears in place of
the prosciutto.

garden pea soup with asparagus & prosciutto croûtes
Prepare the basic recipe, adding a lightly cooked asparagus spear to each
prosciutto croûte.

garden pea soup with smoked salmon croûtes
Prepare the basic recipe, topping each croûte with a strip of smoked salmon
in place of the prosciutto.

garden pea soup with anchovy & quail's egg croûtes
Prepare the basic recipe, omitting the prosciutto and mustard. Boil four
quail's eggs for 4 minutes, then drain, cool and shell. Top each croûte with
a drained anchovy fillet and a halved quail's egg.

garden pea soup with artichoke croûtes
Prepare the basic recipe, using 4 marinated chargrilled artichokes in place
of the prosciutto.

variations

spicy crab & coconut soup

see base recipe page 202

spicy crab & coconut soup with noodles
Prepare the basic recipe. Cook 115 g (4 oz) noodles according to the instructions on the packet, drain and divide among four bowls. Ladle the soup over the top.

spicy crab & coconut soup with rice
Prepare the basic recipe and serve the soup ladled over steamed rice.

spicy prawn & coconut soup
Prepare the basic recipe, using 250 g (9 oz) peeled cooked tiger prawns in place of the crabmeat.

spicy salmon & coconut soup
Prepare the basic recipe, adding 2 skinned, boneless salmon fillets, cut into strips, in place of the crabmeat. Cook for about 2 minutes longer, until the salmon is cooked through.

variations

broad bean & mange tout soup

see base recipe page 204

broad bean & mange tout soup with parmesan cheese
Prepare the basic recipe, sprinkling Parmesan cheese shavings over
each serving.

broad bean & mange tout soup with spinach
Prepare the basic recipe, adding 2 large handfuls of baby spinach leaves
(or shredded large leaves) just before the end of the cooking time.

broad bean & mange tout soup with bacon
Prepare the basic recipe, frying 3 roughly chopped rindless bacon rashers
with the shallots and garlic.

broad bean & mange tout soup with spicy chorizo
Prepare the basic recipe, frying 55 g (2 oz) diced chorizo with the shallots
and garlic.

broad bean & mange tout soup with mint
Prepare the basic recipe, using 1 tablespoon chopped fresh mint in place
of the basil.

variations

creamed artichoke soup with anchovy toasts

see base recipe page 205

creamed artichoke soup with lemon, with anchovy toasts
Prepare the basic recipe, stirring ½ teaspoon grated lemon rind into the soup with the mint.

creamed artichoke soup
Prepare the basic recipe, omitting the anchovy toasts.

creamed artichoke soup with garlic toasts
Prepare the basic recipe, omitting the anchovies and butter. Instead, rub the toasts with a cut clove of garlic and drizzle with a little olive oil.

creamed artichoke soup with chives & anchovy toasts
Prepare the basic recipe, using 2 tablespoons snipped fresh chives in place of the mint.

variations

vermouth & fennel soup

see base recipe page 207

white wine & fennel soup
Prepare the basic recipe, using white wine in place of the vermouth.

vermouth & fennel soup with chives
Prepare the basic recipe, stirring 2 tablespoons snipped fresh chives into the finished soup.

vermouth & celery soup
Prepare the basic recipe, using celery in place of the fennel.

vermouth & fennel soup with rosemary
Prepare the basic recipe, adding a sprig of rosemary to the stock. Simmer, then remove the rosemary before blending.

variations

asparagus soup with smoked salmon crostini

see base recipe page 208

simple cream of asparagus soup
Prepare the basic recipe, omitting the smoked salmon crostini.

asparagus soup with salami crostini
Prepare the basic recipe, topping each crostini with a twist of salami in place of the smoked salmon.

asparagus soup with caviar crostini
Prepare the basic recipe, using soured cream in place of the mayonnaise, and a dollop of caviar in place of each smoked salmon strip.

asparagus soup with smoked trout crostini
Prepare the basic recipe, topping each crostini with a large flake of smoked trout in place of the strip of smoked salmon.

variations

rich porcini soup with sherry & nutmeg

see base recipe page 211

fresh porcini soup
Prepare the basic recipe, omitting the dried porcini and using a mixture of
fresh porcini mushrooms and chestnut mushrooms. The additional fresh
mushrooms will give up their moisture, which is used instead of the soaking
liquid from the dried porcini.

porcini soup with white wine
Prepare the basic recipe, using white wine in place of the sherry.

porcini soup with goat's cheese croûtes
Prepare the basic recipe. To serve, toast 4 slices of baguette until golden on
both sides, then top with goat's cheese and float on each bowl of soup.

porcini soup with walnut & blue cheese toasts
Prepare the basic recipe. To serve, toast 4 slices of walnut bread until golden
on one side. Turn over and top with a sliver of blue cheese and grill until
melting, then serve with the soup.

porcini soup with thyme
Prepare the basic recipe, adding 1 teaspoon fresh thyme leaves with the
stock. Omit the parsley.

variations

sweet pepper & salmon soup with fresh basil

see base recipe page 212

sweet pepper & king prawn soup
Prepare the basic recipe, using 300 g (10½ oz) peeled cooked king prawns in place of the salmon. Add to the soup about 1 minute before serving to warm through.

chilled sweet pepper soup with fresh basil
Prepare the basic recipe, omitting the salmon. Leave to cool, then chill for at least 2 hours before serving.

sweet pepper & salmon soup with fresh chives
Prepare the basic recipe, using 3 tablespoons snipped fresh chives in place of the basil.

sweet pepper & salmon soup with fresh mint
Prepare the basic recipe, using 1 handful of fresh mint leaves in place of the basil.

sweet pepper soup with fresh basil
Prepare the basic recipe, omitting the salmon.

variations

classic beef consommé

see base recipe page 215

chicken consommé
Prepare the basic recipe, using chicken stock in place of the beef stock, and minced chicken in place of the beef.

chilli beef consommé
Prepare the basic recipe, adding 2 seeded, chopped fresh red chillies with the other vegetables.

rich beef consommé with port
Prepare the basic recipe, using port in place of the sherry.

beef consommé with spring onions
Prepare the basic recipe, adding 4 finely sliced spring onions to the consommé just before ladling into bowls.

asian flavours

Light broths with noodles, rich and creamy coconut milk soups and concoctions spiked with fragrant herbs and spices are all traditions found within the Asian kitchen. Try your hand at making any one of these soups and enjoy a taste of the East.

malaysian prawn laksa

see variations page 244

A chunky seafood broth ladled over freshly cooked noodles, this tasty soup makes a superlative meal in a bowl.

2 shallots, chopped
3 red chillies, seeded and chopped
1 garlic clove
2 tsp grated fresh root ginger
Grated rind of 1 lime
1 tsp ground turmeric
1 tsp ground coriander
2 tbsp Thai fish sauce
2 tbsp peanuts

2 tbsp sunflower oil
1 l (1¾ pts) fish or vegetable stock
225 g (8 oz) wheat noodles
200 ml (7 fl oz) coconut cream
1 tsp soft brown sugar
350 g (12 oz) raw tiger prawns, shelled
    and deveined
4 handfuls beansprouts
Large handful of fresh coriander leaves

Process the shallots, chillies, garlic, ginger, lime rind, turmeric, coriander, fish sauce and peanuts to a paste in a food processor. Heat the oil in a large saucepan and fry the paste for 2 minutes. Stir in the stock. Bring to the boil, reduce the heat and simmer for 10 minutes.

Cook the noodles according to the packet instructions. Drain and divide among 4 bowls. Stir the coconut cream and sugar into the broth, add the prawns and simmer for about 2 minutes, until the prawns are pink and cooked. Remove from the heat, stir in the beansprouts and half the coriander. Ladle the broth over the noodles and top with more coriander leaves.

Serves 4

thai-style coconut chicken noodle soup

see variations page 245

This hot, spicy coconut broth ladled over fine wheat noodles makes a delicious, sustaining meal. Try it as a spicy alternative to traditional chicken noodle soup.

2 tbsp sunflower oil
3 shallots, finely chopped
4 green chillies, seeded and chopped
2 tsp grated fresh root ginger
2 garlic cloves, crushed
2 lemongrass stalks, chopped
4 kaffir lime leaves, shredded
400 ml (14 fl oz) coconut milk
800 ml (28 fl oz) chicken stock

2 skinless boneless chicken breasts, cut into
    small bite-size pieces
85 g (3 oz) baby corn, quartered lengthways
200 g (7 oz) fine wheat noodles
1 to 2 tbsp Thai fish sauce
Juice of about 1 lime, to taste
Bunch of spring onions, sliced
Handful of fresh coriander

Heat the oil in a saucepan. Add the shallots, chillies, ginger and garlic. Cook for 3 minutes. Stir in the lemongrass, lime leaves, coconut milk and stock. Boil, then reduce the heat, add the chicken and simmer gently for 10 minutes. Add the corn and cook for 2 to 3 minutes.

Meanwhile, cook the noodles according to the packet instructions, drain and divide among 4 bowls. Add fish sauce and lime juice to taste to the soup. Stir in the spring onions and half the coriander. Ladle the soup over the noodles and sprinkle with the remaining coriander.

Serves 4

miso broth with ramen & seared tuna

see variations page 246

This light Japanese broth is poured over tender ramen noodles (fine, quick-cooking wheat noodles) and topped with seared tuna to make a healthy and delicious meal.

1 l (1¾ pts) water
4 tbsp miso paste
250 g (9 oz) ramen noodles
4 tuna steaks (each about 115 g / 4 oz)

Salt and ground black pepper
Groundnut or sunflower oil, for greasing
4 spring onions, sliced

Heat the water and miso paste gently in a large saucepan, stirring until the miso has dissolved. Bring to the boil, then reduce the heat, cover and simmer gently while preparing the remaining ingredients.

Cook the noodles according to the packet instructions, drain and divide among four bowls. Season the tuna steaks with salt and ground black pepper. Brush a non-stick frying pan with oil and heat until hot. Sear the tuna for about 2 minutes on each side until cooked, but still pink in the middle. Place a tuna steak in each bowl and scatter with spring onions.

Ladle the broth into the bowls and serve immediately.

Serves 4

red curry soup with duck

see variations page 247

The distinctive, meaty flavour and firm texture of duck makes a good base for the flavours of a classic Thai red curry in this wholesome soup.

2 tbsp sunflower oil
2 shallots, finely chopped
2 fresh red chillies, seeded and chopped
2 tsp grated fresh ginger
2 tsp Thai red curry paste
1.2 l (2 pts) chicken stock
2 skinless boneless duck breasts, cut into
   bite-size strips

120 ml (4 fl oz) coconut cream
1 tsp soft brown sugar
Juice of about 1 lime, to taste
1 tbsp Thai fish sauce
1 green pepper, seeded and sliced
1 red pepper, seeded and sliced
55 g (2 oz) baby corn, quartered
Handful of basil leaves, to serve

Heat the oil in a large saucepan. Add the shallots, chillies and ginger, and cook for 2 minutes. Stir in the curry paste and fry for a further 2 minutes. Add the stock and duck, and bring to the boil. Reduce the heat, cover and simmer for about 15 minutes.

Stir in the coconut cream, sugar, lime juice and fish sauce to taste. Add the vegetables and simmer for 2 minutes, until just tender but retaining a crisp bite.

Ladle the soup into bowls, scatter with the basil leaves and serve.

Serves 4

vietnamese beef noodle soup

see variations page 248

Based on the classic soup served by Vietnamese street vendors, this broth is refreshing, yet substantial. The wafer-thin slices of beef are cooked very lightly in the hot stock.

1.2 l (2 pts) good-quality fresh beef stock
2 tsp grated fresh root ginger
4 cloves
1 cinnamon sticks
4 star anise
1 tsp black peppercorns
1 tbsp fish sauce
200 g (7 oz) flat rice noodles

250 g (9 oz) beef sirloin, cut into
    wafer-thin slices
2 red chillies, seeded and finely sliced
Bunch of spring onions, sliced
2 handfuls of beansprouts
Large handful of fresh coriander leaves
1 lime, quartered

Put the stock in a large saucepan. Add the ginger, cloves, cinnamon, star anise, peppercorns and fish sauce, and bring to the boil. Reduce the heat, cover and simmer for about 1 hour.

Strain the stock into a clean saucepan and heat until simmering. Put the noodles in a bowl, pour boiling water over them. Leave to stand for 5 minutes until tender, then drain and divide among four bowls.

Add the beef to the noodles in the serving bowls. Sprinkle with the chillies, spring onions and beansprouts. Ladle over the hot stock, sprinkle with the coriander and serve, with the lime wedges for squeezing.

Serves 4

hot-and-sour crab soup

see variations page 249

Fresh and fiery, this deliciously fragrant soup makes a lively light lunch or appetiser. If you prefer milder flavours, simply use fewer chillies.

2 shallots, finely chopped
2 garlic cloves, crushed
2 tsp grated fresh root ginger
3 red bird's eye chillies, seeded and finely
    chopped, plus 1 seeded and shredded
1 tbsp sweet chilli sauce
4 kaffir lime leaves, shredded
1.2 l (2 pts) fish or vegetable stock

2 tsp soft brown sugar
Juice of 1 lime
1 tsp Thai fish sauce
Two 170-g (6-oz) cans white crabmeat
4 handfuls beansprouts
5 spring onions, sliced
Handful of fresh coriander leaves

Put the shallots, garlic, ginger, chillies, chilli sauce, lime leaves and stock in a large saucepan. Bring to the boil, then reduce the heat, cover and simmer for about 20 minutes.

Strain the stock into a clean saucepan and stir in the sugar, lime juice and fish sauce. Divide the crabmeat among four bowls. Top each portion with a handful of beansprouts and sprinkle over the spring onions and shredded chilli. Ladle over the stock, sprinkle with coriander leaves and serve immediately.

Serves 4

fiery thai broth with tofu & spring onions

see variations page 250

Hot, light and fragrant, laden with tender green cabbage and healthy tofu, this full-flavoured broth makes a delicious start to an Asian-style meal.

2 tbsp sunflower oil
3 green bird's eye chillies, seeded and chopped
2 tsp Thai green curry paste
1.2 l (2 pts) vegetable stock
4 kaffir lime leaves, shredded
2 tsp soft brown sugar

Juice of 1 lime, or to taste
100 g (3½ oz) cabbage, shredded
150 g (5 oz) deep-fried tofu, cubed
Bunch of spring onions, sliced
Handful of fresh coriander leaves

Heat the oil in a large saucepan. Add the chillies and curry paste, and fry for about 30 seconds. Pour in the stock and add the lime leaves, then bring to the boil. Reduce the heat, cover and simmer for about 20 minutes.

Strain the broth into a clean saucepan and stir in the sugar and lime juice to taste. Add the cabbage and simmer for about 1 minute, then add the tofu and cook for 30 to 60 seconds, until the cabbage is just tender.

Ladle the soup into bowls, scatter with spring onions and coriander, and serve.

Serves 4

chinese-style broth with wontons

see variations page 251

This simple, fragrant broth, highlighted with the smoky flavour of sesame, makes a delicious light meal or appetiser.

for the wontons

1 tbsp sunflower oil
1 tsp sesame oil
½ small onion, grated
5 drained canned water chestnuts, finely chopped
55 g (2 oz) minced pork
16 wonton wrappers
1 tsp soy sauce

Ground black pepper

for the broth

1.2 l (2 pts) vegetable stock
3 tbsp mirin or sherry
1 tsp soft brown sugar
2 tsp soy sauce
1 tsp sesame oil
4 spring onions, sliced

For the wontons, heat the oils in a small non-stick frying pan. Stir-fry the onion, chestnuts and pork for 3 minutes, until the pork is cooked. Mix in the soy sauce and black pepper. Lay a wonton wrapper on a board and dampen the edges. Put a teaspoonful of filling in the centre, gather up the wrapper and twist it to seal the filling in a little purse. Repeat with the remaining ingredients. Cook the wontons in a steamer for 12 minutes, until tender.

Meanwhile, bring the stock to the boil in a large saucepan. Reduce the heat and stir in the mirin or sherry, sugar, soy sauce and sesame oil. Put four wontons in each bowl, ladle the hot soup over them, scatter with spring onions and serve.

Serves 4

hot sichuan-style noodle soup with coriander omelette

see variations page 252

This hot and spicy, colourful broth is ladled over rice noodles and topped with strips of fragrant omelette. It makes a delicious light meal or appetiser.

115 g (4 oz) fine rice noodles
1.2 l (2 pts) chicken or vegetable stock
2 tsp grated fresh root ginger
1 fresh red bird's eye chilli, seeded and
    finely chopped
1 tsp freshly ground black pepper
1 tbsp tomato purée

1 tbsp soy sauce
1 tbsp rice vinegar
1 egg
Handful of fresh coriander, chopped
1 tbsp sunflower oil
85 g (3 oz) sliced bamboo shoots, drained
5 spring onions, sliced

Soak the noodles in a bowl of boiling water for 5 minutes. Drain and snip into 6-cm (2½-in) lengths, then set aside. Bring the stock, ginger, chilli, black pepper, tomato purée, soy sauce and vinegar to the boil in a large saucepan. Reduce the heat and simmer for 5 minutes.

Meanwhile, beat the egg and stir in the coriander. Heat the oil in a small frying pan, add the egg and swirl it around the pan into a thin layer. Cook for 2 minutes, until set. Slide the omelette on to a board. Roll up and thinly slice the omelette, then shake out into strips. Add the noodles and bamboo shoots to the soup and heat for 1 minute. Ladle the soup into bowls, sprinkle with spring onions and top with omelette.

Serves 4

vietnamese-style sour fish soup

see variations page 253

Hot and spicy, with succulent fish, juicy pineapple and crisp beansprouts, this soup is delicious at any time of day.

2 tbsp vegetable oil
2 shallots, finely chopped
2 garlic cloves, crushed
2 tsp grated fresh root ginger
2 hot red chillies, seeded and chopped
2 lemongrass stalks, chopped
1.2 l (2 pts) vegetable stock
2 tsp tamarind paste
1 tbsp soft brown sugar

1 tsp fish sauce
4 tomatoes, peeled and chopped
200 g (7 oz) peeled, cored, fresh pineapple, cut into bite-size pieces
500 g (1 lb 2 oz) firm white fish, skinned and cut into bite-size pieces
2 handfuls beansprouts
Handful of fresh coriander leaves

Heat the oil in a large saucepan. Add the shallots, garlic, ginger and chillies, and cook for about 2 minutes. Add the lemongrass and stock and bring to the boil. Reduce the heat, cover and simmer for about 30 minutes.

Strain the stock into a clean saucepan and stir in the tamarind paste, sugar and fish sauce. Add the tomatoes and pineapple, and simmer for about 3 minutes. Add the fish and simmer for a further 2 to 3 minutes, until cooked through.

Ladle the soup into bowls. Top with beansprouts and coriander, and serve immediately

Serves 4

variations

malaysian prawn laksa

see base recipe page 227

malaysian salmon laksa
Prepare the basic recipe, using 3 skinned, cubed salmon fillets in place of
the prawns.

malaysian prawn laksa with rice noodles
Prepare the basic recipe, using flat rice noodles in place of wheat noodles.

malaysian prawn laksa with spring onions
Prepare the basic recipe, adding 1 bunch of sliced spring onions with
the beansprouts.

vegetarian laksa
Prepare the basic recipe omitting the fish sauce and prawns, and seasoning
with salt. Add 300 g (10½ oz) cubed tofu and warm through for 1 minute
before adding the beansprouts and coriander.

malaysian chicken laksa
Prepare the basic recipe, adding 2 skinless, boneless chicken breasts, sliced
into small bite-size pieces, with the stock and coconut milk.

thai-style coconut chicken noodle soup

see base recipe page 229

thai-style coconut prawn noodle soup
Prepare the basic recipe, omitting the chicken. Add 300 g (10½ oz) shelled, deveined raw tiger prawns 2 minutes before the end of cooking and simmer until pink and cooked through.

thai-style coconut tofu noodle soup
Prepare the basic recipe, omitting the chicken. Add 300 g (10½ oz) deep-fried tofu cubes with the spring onions.

thai-style coconut crab noodle soup
Prepare the basic recipe, omitting the chicken. Add two 170-g (6-oz) cans white crabmeat with the spring onions.

thai-style coconut vegetable noodle soup
Prepare the basic recipe, omitting the chicken. Add 1 seeded, sliced red pepper, a large handful of halved button mushrooms and 85 g (3 oz) broccoli florets with the corn.

thai-style coconut fish soup
Prepare the basic recipe, omitting the chicken. Add 300 g (10½ oz) cubed, skinned, firm white fish 2 to 3 minutes before the end of cooking.

variations

miso broth with ramen & seared tuna

see base recipe page 230

miso broth with ramen & tofu
Prepare the basic recipe, omitting the tuna. Add 250 g (9 oz) cubed silken tofu to the broth and warm through for 1 minute, then ladle into bowls and sprinkle with the spring onions.

miso broth with ramen & seared salmon
Prepare the basic recipe, using skinned salmon fillets in place of the tuna steaks. Sear on each side for about 4 minutes, until cooked, then finish as in the main recipe.

miso broth with ramen & king prawns
Prepare the basic recipe, omitting the tuna steaks. Add 350 g (12 oz) shelled, deveined raw tiger prawns to the broth 2 minutes before serving. Cook until pink and cooked through, then ladle over the noodles.

miso broth with ramen & chargrilled chicken
Slice 3 skinless, boneless chicken breasts into strips. Combine 2 crushed garlic cloves, 1 tablespoon sunflower oil and salt and pepper. Toss with the chicken and marinate for 1 hour. Prepare the basic recipe, omitting the tuna. Heat a ridged griddle pan, then cook the chicken for about 2 minutes on each side. Scatter over the cooked noodles and ladle over the broth.

variations

red curry soup with duck

see base recipe page 232

red curry soup with duck & steamed rice
Prepare the basic recipe. To serve, place a couple of heaped spoonfuls of
steamed Jasmine rice in the bottom of each bowl before ladling in the soup.

red curry soup with chicken
Prepare the basic recipe, using skinless boneless chicken breasts in place of
the duck.

red curry soup with prawns
Prepare the basic recipe, omitting the duck. Add 350 g (12 oz) peeled,
deveined raw tiger prawns with the vegetables and cook until they are pink
and cooked.

red curry soup with tofu
Prepare the basic recipe, omitting the duck. Add 250 g (9 oz) deep-fried tofu
cubes with the vegetables.

variations

vietnamese beef noodle soup

see base recipe page 233

vietnamese chicken noodle soup
Prepare the basic recipe, using chicken stock in place of the beef stock, and 2 sliced, skinless cooked chicken breasts in place of the beef.

vietnamese pork noodle soup
Prepare the basic recipe, using chicken stock in place of the beef stock, and 2 sliced, cooked pork loin steaks in place of the beef.

vietnamese prawn noodle soup
Prepare the basic recipe, using fish or vegetable stock in place of the beef stock, and 250 g (9 oz) cooked, peeled tiger prawns in place of the beef.

vietnamese crab noodle soup
Prepare the basic recipe, using fish or vegetable stock in place of the beef stock, and using two 170-g (6-oz) cans white crabmeat in place of the beef.

variations

hot-and-sour crab soup

see base recipe page 235

hot-and-sour crab soup with noodles
Prepare the basic recipe. Towards the end of cooking time, soak 115 g (4 oz) rice noodles in boiling water for 5 minutes, then drain and divide among the four bowls. Continue as in the main recipe.

hot-and-sour chicken soup
Prepare the basic recipe, using 2 sliced, skinless cooked chicken breasts in place of the crabmeat.

hot-and-sour prawn soup
Prepare the basic recipe, using 250 g (9 oz) peeled cooked tiger prawns in place of the crabmeat.

hot-and-sour tofu soup
Prepare the basic recipe, using 250 g (9 oz) cubed silken tofu in place of the crabmeat.

hot-and-sour shiitake mushroom soup
Prepare the basic recipe, adding 6 quartered fresh shiitake mushrooms to the strained stock and simmering for 4 minutes. Continue as in the main recipe, omitting the crabmeat.

variations

fiery thai broth with tofu & spring onions

see base recipe page 236

fiery thai broth with tofu & vegetables
Prepare the basic recipe, adding 1 large carrot, cut into thin batons, with
the tofu. Put a handful of baby spinach leaves in each bowl before adding
the soup.

fiery thai broth with tofu, cauliflower & spring onions
Prepare the basic recipe, adding 100 g (3½ oz) bite-size cauliflower florets in
place of the cabbage.

fiery thai broth with tofu, broccoli & spring onions
Prepare the basic recipe, adding 100 g (3½ oz) bite-size broccoli florets in
place of the cabbage.

fiery thai broth with smoked mackerel & spring onions
Skin 2 smoked mackerel fillets and break the flesh into large flakes,
discarding any bones. Prepare the basic recipe, adding the smoked mackerel
in place of the tofu.

fiery thai broth with tofu, spring onions & jasmine rice
Prepare the basic recipe, spooning a couple of tablespoons of steamed
Jasmine rice into each bowl before ladling in the soup.

variations

chinese-style broth with wontons

see base recipe page 239

chinese-style broth with crispy wontons
Prepare the basic recipe. Instead of steaming the wontons, deep-fry them
for about 4 minutes until golden, in oil heated to 190°C (375°F). Drain on
paper towels before putting in the bowls.

chinese-style broth with tofu
Prepare the basic recipe, omitting the wontons. Add 250 g (9 oz) tofu to the
stock and warm through just before serving.

chinese-style broth with carrots & spring onions
Prepare the basic recipe, omitting the wontons and simmering 1 large carrot,
cut into thin batons, in the soup for 2 minutes before serving.

chinese-style broth with chicken wontons
Prepare the basic recipe, using minced chicken in place of the pork.

chinese-style broth with cabbage
Prepare the basic recipe, adding 100 g (3½ oz) shredded cabbage to the
broth 1 to 2 minutes before serving. Simmer until just tender.

variations

hot sichuan-style noodle soup with coriander omelette

see base recipe page 240

hot sichuan-style chicken noodle soup with coriander omelette
Prepare the basic recipe, adding 2 shredded, cooked, skinless chicken breasts
with the noodles and bamboo shoots.

hot sichuan-style noodle soup with tofu, & coriander omelette
Prepare the basic recipe, adding 250 g (9 oz) cubed silken tofu with the
noodles and bamboo shoots.

hot sichuan-style noodle soup with cabbage, & coriander omelette
Prepare the basic recipe, adding 100 g (3½ oz) shredded cabbage to
the stock and simmering for 3 minutes before adding the noodles and
bamboo shoots.

hot sichuan-style noodle soup with red pepper, & coriander omelette
Prepare the basic recipe, adding 1 seeded red pepper, cut into fine strips,
with the noodles and bamboo shoots.

variations

vietnamese-style sour fish soup

see base recipe page 243

vietnamese-style sour prawn soup
Prepare the basic recipe, using 350 g (12 oz) peeled raw tiger prawns in
place of the fish.

vietnamese-style sour fish soup with bamboo shoots
Prepare the basic recipe, adding 100 g (3½ oz) sliced bamboo shoots with the
fish.

vietnamese-style sour tofu soup
Prepare the basic recipe, adding 250 g (9 oz) cubed silken tofu in place of
the fish. Simmer for 1 minute, then serve.

vietnamese-style sour chicken soup
Prepare the basic recipe, adding 3 skinless cooked chicken breasts, cut into
bite-size pieces, in place of the fish.

vietnamese-style sour fish soup with mango
Prepare the basic recipe, using 2 small peeled, stoned mangoes, cut into
bite-size chunks, in place of the pineapple.

fruity flavours

Most people think of vegetables, meat, poultry and seafood when they think of soup but soups made with fruits are wonderful too, whether it's a simple soup flavoured with orange or a sweet, fruity soup you could serve for dessert.

spiced chicken & apricot soup

see variations page 274

Tangy and light, yet fragrant and fruity with cinnamon and apricot, this soup makes a lively alternative to plain chicken noodle soup when you need a little comfort.

2 tbsp olive oil
1 onion, finely chopped
3 garlic cloves, crushed
2 skinless, boneless chicken breasts, cut into
    bite-size strips
1.2 l (2 pts) chicken stock

2 tsp ground cinnamon
1 tsp ground ginger
115 g (4 oz) ready-to-eat dried apricots, chopped
Salt and ground black pepper
2 tbsp chopped fresh parsley, plus extra
    to garnish

Heat the oil in a large saucepan. Add the onion and garlic, and cook gently for 4 minutes. Add the chicken, then pour in the stock, and stir in the cinnamon, ginger and apricots.

Bring the soup to the boil. Reduce the heat, cover the saucepan and simmer the soup for 20 minutes, until the chicken is cooked.

Add salt and pepper to taste. Sprinkle in the parsley and ladle the soup into bowls to serve.

Serves 4

cock-a-leekie with tender prunes

see variations page 275

This classic Scottish soup is a real meal in a bowl. Adding barley ensures it's sufficiently sustaining to ward off hunger pangs between meals.

100 g (3½ oz) pearl barley
1.2 l (2 pts) chicken stock
1 tsp dried thyme
5 juniper berries, crushed
3 large leeks, trimmed and sliced

115 g (4 oz) ready-to-eat dried prunes, cut into bite-size pieces
350 g (12 oz) cooked chicken, cut into bite-size pieces
Ground black pepper

Put the barley, stock, thyme and juniper berries in a large saucepan. Bring to the boil, stir well, then reduce the heat and cover the saucepan. Simmer the soup for about 25 minutes, until the barley is tender.

Add the leeks, prunes and chicken to the soup. Re-cover and simmer for about 10 minutes, until the leeks are tender. Season with black pepper and ladle the soup into bowls.

Serves 4

hungarian cherry soup

see variations page 276

This sweet-sour cherry soup is rich and creamy, and traditionally served in small portions as an elegant appetiser. Instead of bowls, try serving the soup in stylish cups on saucers.

900 g (2 lb) Morello cherries, stoned
140 g (5 oz) caster sugar
2 cinnamon sticks
400 ml (14 fl oz) red wine

400 ml (14 fl oz) water
120 ml (4 fl oz) single cream
Lemon juice, to taste
Crème fraîche, to serve

Put the cherries in a large saucepan and sprinkle with the sugar. Tuck in the cinnamon sticks and pour in the wine and water. Bring to the boil, then reduce the heat, cover and simmer for about 20 minutes.

Remove the cinnamon sticks. Stir in the single cream, then check the flavour, adding a squeeze of lemon juice to taste. Ladle the soup into small bowls and serve topped with crème fraîche.

Serves 4

chilled melon soup

see variations page 277

Choose ripe, fragrant melons for this simple, refreshing summer appetiser — the more fabulous the flavour of the melons, the better the soup.

3 cantaloupe melons
Juice of 3 oranges

Juice of ½ to 1 lime, to taste
Fresh mint leaves, to garnish

Cut the melons in half and scoop out the seeds. Scoop the flesh into a food processor or blender. Add the orange juice and process until smooth.

Pour the soup into a large bowl and stir in lime juice to taste. Chill for at least 2 hours. Ladle the soup into bowls and serve garnished with fresh mint leaves.

Serves 4

greek egg & lemon soup

see variations page 278

This classic soup is known as avgolemono in Greece. It is sharp, creamy and packed with tiny rice-shaped pasta (orzo) and thickened with eggs.

1.2 l (2 pts) vegetable or chicken stock
100 g (3½ oz) orzo
3 eggs

Juice of 1 lemon
Salt and ground black pepper
Chopped fresh parsley, to garnish

Pour the stock into a large saucepan and bring to the boil. Add the orzo and cook for about 5 minutes, until tender. Remove the saucepan from the heat.

Beat the eggs with the lemon juice and 1 tablespoon cold water, then gradually beat in a couple of ladlefuls of the hot stock. Stirring constantly, pour the egg mixture back into the saucepan of soup.

Remove the saucepan from the heat. Add salt and pepper to taste and ladle the soup into bowls. Sprinkle with chopped fresh parsley and serve.

Serves 4

pear & blue cheese soup with prosciutto crisps

see variations page 279

Tangy blue cheese and sweet, tender pear may sound an unlikely combination, but the result is sublime in this richly flavoured soup. Serve it as an elegant appetiser.

2 tbsp sunflower oil
1 onion, chopped
1 garlic clove, crushed
4 pears, peeled, cored and chopped

750 ml (1¼ pts) vegetable stock
85 g (3 oz) blue cheese
4 strips prosciutto
Ground black pepper

Heat the oil in a large saucepan. Add the onion and garlic, and cook gently for 4 minutes. Add the pears and stock and bring to the boil. Reduce the heat, cover the saucepan and simmer for about 5 minutes, until the pears are tender.

Pour the soup into a food processor or blender, add the cheese and process until smooth. Season to taste with pepper and keep warm.

Preheat the grill. Lay the prosciutto on a rack in a grill pan and grill until crisp. Snip the crisp strips into bite-size pieces. Ladle the soup into serving bowls, sprinkle with the prosciutto crisps and serve immediately.

Serves 4

spicy chicken soup with chilli & lime

see variations page 280

Unlike many fruit soups, which have a sweet flavour, the lime gives this soup a wonderfully sour, zesty flavour that complements the aromatic spices and basil.

2 tbsp sunflower oil
2 shallots, finely chopped
3 garlic cloves, crushed
1 tsp grated fresh root ginger
3 green chillies, seeded and finely chopped

1.2 l (2 pts) chicken stock
300 g (10½ oz) skinless cooked chicken, cut
    into small bite-size pieces
Grated rind and juice of 1 lime
Handful of fresh basil leaves, torn

Heat the oil in a large saucepan. Add the shallots, garlic, ginger and chillies, and cook for about 2 minutes. Pour in the stock and bring to the boil. Reduce the heat, cover the saucepan and simmer for about 15 minutes.

Add the chicken to the soup and simmer for a further 1 to 2 minutes. Stir in the lime rind and juice. Ladle the soup into serving bowls, sprinkle with basil and serve immediately.

Serves 4

strawberry and chilli soup

see variations page 281

Served in small bowls, this fiery, refreshing soup makes a deliciously unusual appetiser.
It takes only minutes to prepare and is perfect for entertaining.

675 g (1½ lb) ripe strawberries, hulled
Juice of 3 oranges
1½ red chillies, seeded and chopped

Salt
Ice cubes, to serve (optional)
Fresh mint leaves, to garnish

Process the strawberries, orange juice and chillies in a food processor or blender and until
smooth. Add a pinch of salt and pulse to mix it in.

Pour the soup into small bowls, add a couple of ice cubes to each portion, if liked, and serve
garnished with mint.

Serves 4

fish & orange soup

see variations page 282

This light, fragrant citrus broth, with chunks of firm white fish, makes a stylish light meal, served with chunks of crusty bread.

2 tbsp sunflower oil
1 onion, finely chopped
2 garlic cloves, crushed
1.2 l (2 pts) fish stock
½ tsp sweet paprika
1 tbsp tomato purée

500 g (1 lb 2 oz) firm white fish fillets, skinned and cubed
1 tsp finely grated orange rind
Juice of 2 oranges
Handful of chopped fresh parsley
Salt and ground black pepper

Heat the oil in a large saucepan. Add the onion and garlic, and cook for about 4 minutes. Stir in the stock, paprika and tomato purée, and simmer for about 5 minutes. Add the fish, orange rind and juice, and simmer for 2 to 3 minutes, until the fish is just cooked.

Season the soup with salt and pepper to taste, then ladle it into serving bowls and scatter with fresh parsley. Serve immediately.

Serves 4

duck & pomegranate soup

see variations page 283

Sweet, yet astringent, pomegranate and fruity, full-bodied port come together beautifully in this richly flavoured soup.

2 boneless duck breasts
Salt and ground black pepper
2 shallots, finely chopped
2 garlic cloves, crushed
2 tbsp plain flour

1 l (1¾ pts) chicken or duck stock
2 pomegranates
120 ml (4 fl oz) port
Handful of parsley, chopped

Score the duck skin in a lattice pattern and rub with salt. Heat a large non-stick saucepan. Add the duck, skin down, and cook for 10 minutes. Pour away most of the fat, leaving about 2 tablespoons in the pan, turn the duck and cook for 4 to 5 minutes. Remove and set aside. Add the shallots and garlic. Cook gently for 2 to 3 minutes. Stir in the flour and cook for 1 minute. Gradually stir in the stock. Boil, reduce the heat, cover and simmer for 10 minutes.

Meanwhile, halve the pomegranates. Hold one half over a bowl and sharply tap the back of the peel with a wooden spoon to remove the seeds. Repeat with the remaining fruit. Reserve a quarter of the seeds. Put the remaining seeds in a sieve over a bowl, and press with a spoon to extract the juice. Stir the juice and port into the soup, and season to taste.

Slice the duck into thin strips, add to the soup and warm through. Serve sprinkled with parsley and the reserved pomegranate seeds.

Serves 4

variations

spiced chicken & apricot soup

see base recipe page 255

spiced chicken & prune soup
Prepare the basic recipe, using ready-to-eat dried prunes in place of
the apricots.

spiced chicken & apricot soup with couscous
Prepare the basic recipe. To serve, soak 140 g (5 oz) couscous in 175 ml
(6 fl oz) boiling water for 5 minutes. Fluff up with a fork and add
1 tablespoon olive oil and a handful of chopped fresh parsley, then
toss to combine. Spoon the couscous into each bowl of soup.

spiced chicken & apricot soup with honey
Prepare the basic recipe, stirring 2 teaspoons clear honey into the soup with
the dried apricots.

spiced chicken soup with peppers & apricots
Prepare the basic recipe, adding 2 seeded yellow peppers, cut into chunks, to
the soup with the apricots.

spiced chicken noodle soup with apricots
Prepare the basic recipe, adding 115 g (4 oz) vermicelli to the soup about
3 minutes before the end of cooking time. Simmer until tender.

variations

cock-a-leekie with tender prunes

see base recipe page 257

simple cock-a-leekie with tender prunes
Prepare the basic recipe, omitting the barley.

simple cock-a-leekie with rice
Prepare the basic recipe, omitting the barley. Put a couple of spoonfuls of cooked rice in each bowl and ladle over the soup.

rich herb cock-a-leekie with tender prunes
Prepare the basic recipe, adding 1 bay leaf and 2 tablespoons chopped fresh parsley with the thyme. Sprinkle snipped fresh chives over the soup before serving.

vegetarian quorn cock-a-leekie with tender prunes
Prepare the basic recipe, using vegetable stock in place of chicken stock, and Quorn pieces in place of the chicken.

chunky bean cock-a-leekie with tender prunes
Prepare the basic recipe, adding a 400-g (14-oz) can drained and rinsed mixed beans with the leeks, prunes and chicken.

variations

hungarian cherry soup

see base recipe page 258

chilled hungarian cherry soup
Prepare the basic recipe. Leave the soup to cool, then chill it for at least 3 hours before serving.

hungarian cherry soup with port
Prepare the basic recipe, using 300 ml (½ pt) red wine and 120 ml (4 fl oz) port instead of all red wine.

ginger-spiced cherry soup
Prepare the basic recipe, adding 1½ teaspoons ground ginger with the cinnamon sticks.

cherry & vanilla soup
Prepare the basic recipe, adding 1 teaspoon vanilla essence with the single cream.

cherry & almond soup
Prepare the basic recipe, adding 1 teaspoon almond essence with the single cream, and sprinkling the finished soup with toasted slivered almonds.

variations

chilled melon soup

see base recipe page 261

chilled watermelon soup
Prepare the basic recipe, using 2 kg (4½ lb) watermelon in place of the cantaloupe melon.

chilled honeydew soup
Prepare the basic recipe, using 2 kg (4½ lb) honeydew melon in place of the cantaloupe melon.

chilled melon & ginger soup
Prepare the basic recipe, adding 1 teaspoon grated fresh root ginger to the food processor or blender with the melon.

chilled melon soup with mango sorbet
Prepare the basic recipe, adding a scoop of mango sorbet to each bowl of soup when serving.

greek egg & lemon soup

see base recipe page 262

greek egg & lemon soup with chives
Prepare the basic recipe, sprinkling the finished soup with chives instead of parsley.

greek egg & lemon soup with cauliflower
Cut half a small cauliflower into bite-size florets. Prepare the basic recipe, adding the cauliflower with the orzo.

greek egg & lemon soup with spinach
Prepare the basic recipe, stirring 2 large handfuls of baby spinach leaves into the stock before adding the egg mixture.

greek egg & lemon soup with chicken
Prepare the basic recipe, adding 300 g (10½ oz) skinless cooked chicken, cut into small bite-size pieces, just before the end of cooking.

greek egg & lemon soup with lettuce
Prepare the basic recipe, adding 1 shredded Cos lettuce to the stock about a minute before stirring in the egg mixture.

variations

pear & blue cheese soup with prosciutto crisps

see base recipe page 265

pear & goat's cheese soup with prosciutto crisps
Prepare the basic recipe, using goat's cheese in place of the blue cheese.

apple & blue cheese soup with prosciutto crisps
Prepare the basic recipe, using apples in place of the pears.

pear & blue cheese soup with prosciutto crisps & fresh mint
Prepare the basic recipe, sprinkling the soup with chopped fresh mint before serving.

pear & blue cheese soup with garlic toasts
Prepare the basic recipe, omitting the prosciutto. To serve, toast 8 slices of baguette until golden on both sides, then rub with a halved clove of garlic and drizzle with olive oil. Serve with the soup.

variations

spicy chicken soup with chilli & lime

see base recipe page 266

spicy chicken soup with chilli, lime & spring onions
Prepare the basic recipe, adding a bunch of spring onions, sliced, to the soup just before ladling into bowls.

spicy chicken noodle soup with chilli & lime
Prepare the basic recipe, adding 115 g (4 oz) vermicelli to the soup with the chicken. Simmer until the noodles are tender, then ladle into bowls.

spicy prawn soup with chilli & lime
Prepare the basic recipe, omitting the chicken and adding 300 g (10½ oz) deveined, shelled raw tiger prawns instead. Simmer until the prawns are pink and cooked through.

spicy tofu soup with chilli & lime
Prepare the basic recipe, omitting the chicken and adding 250 g (9 oz) cubed silken tofu instead.

spicy fish soup with chilli & lime
Prepare the basic recipe, omitting the chicken and adding 300 g (10½ oz) cubed raw white fish instead. Simmer until the fish is just cooked through.

variations

strawberry & chilli soup

see base recipe page 269

strawberry & chilli soup with red wine soup
Prepare the basic recipe, adding 240 ml (8 fl oz) fruity red wine in place of
the orange juice.

chilled strawberry, pineapple & chilli soup
Prepare the basic recipe, using 240 ml (8 fl oz) pineapple juice in place of
the orange juice.

chilled strawberry, mango & chilli soup
Prepare the basic recipe, using half the quantity of strawberries and
replacing them with the flesh of two ripe, peeled and stoned mangoes.

chilled strawberry, apple & chilli soup
Prepare the basic recipe, using 240 ml (8 fl oz) apple juice in place of the
orange juice.

chilled strawberry & champagne soup
Prepare the basic recipe, omitting the chilli and using 240 ml (8 fl oz)
champagne or sparkling wine in place of the orange juice.

variations

fish & orange soup

see base recipe page 270

fish & orange soup with chorizo
Prepare the basic recipe, frying 55 g (2 oz) diced chorizo sausage with the onion and garlic.

prawn & orange soup
Prepare the basic recipe, using 350 g (12 oz) shelled, deveined, raw tiger prawns in place of the fish.

fish & orange soup with noodles
Prepare the basic recipe, adding 115 g (4 oz) vermicelli to the soup with the fish.

crab & orange soup
Prepare the basic recipe, adding two 170-g (6-oz) cans white crabmeat in place of the fish.

variations

duck & pomegranate soup

see base recipe page 273

duck & orange soup
Prepare the basic recipe, omitting the pomegranates. Stir in 1 teaspoon finely grated orange rind and the juice of 2 oranges, and add a squeeze of lemon juice to taste.

duck & pomegranate soup with red wine
Prepare the basic recipe, using red wine in place of the port.

cream of duck & pomegranate soup
Prepare the basic recipe, stirring 6 tbsp double cream into the soup just before serving.

duck & pomegranate soup with herbs
Prepare the basic recipe, adding 1 bay leaf and 3 fresh thyme sprigs with the stock.

index